ASTROLOGY

Your Personal Guide

SASHA FENTON

WELLFLEET
PRESS

CONTENTS

1

WHAT CONSTITUTES ASTROLOGY?

Astrology isn't a religion or a belief. It's a system that is part astronomical, part psychological, and part forecasting, but unlike many other forms of divination that have come and gone over the centuries, astrology retains its popularity, for the simple reason that it works.

Newspaper astrology deals with each of the twelve "sun signs" because the earth's orbit around the sun is the same each year, so it is easy for a newspaper to put the dates for the sun signs into their stars column. The person reading the paper can immediately see which sun sign applies to him without having to consult an astrologer. Despite the fact that this form of astrology is limited, it remains popular and can be surprisingly useful. "Real astrology" is a different matter, because one needs a birth chart that is based on a person's date and place of birth, and if available, also their time of birth. A birth chart is a map of the solar system at the moment when someone or something comes into being, but an astrologer can easily move the chart forward from its original position in order to plot the trends and events of a person's life as time goes on.

It can be extremely revealing to have a birth chart drawn up and explained, because it brings a level of awareness about the way we project ourselves to others and the way we feel on an inner level. This awareness makes it easier for us to understand ourselves and others. It is also handy to see how the planets will affect our lives on a day-to-day basis.

Astrology isn't hard to learn and it isn't necessary to spend a fortune on specialized software, because there are now many apps and inexpensive forms of software that will give you the basic birth chart and some useful data. At the time of writing, I have an app on my phone that cost me £3, which is about $5, and it does a perfectly good job, even giving a brief interpretation of the planets and the placement on any particular astrological chart. However, I have plenty of good-quality astrological software as well.

Included in this book is a wall chart that serves as a quick go-to guide about the major components of astrology.

Astrology means "the study of the stars."

Horoscope means "map of the hour."

Zodiac means "a circle of animals."

The Components

Natal Astrology

The natal, or birth, chart shows the character, personality, and psychology.

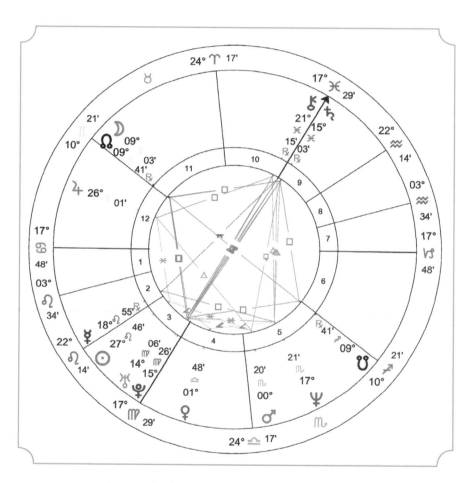

An example of a natal chart, also known as a birth chart.

Predictive Astrology

This shows the trends and events by the movement of the planets in relation to the original birth chart.

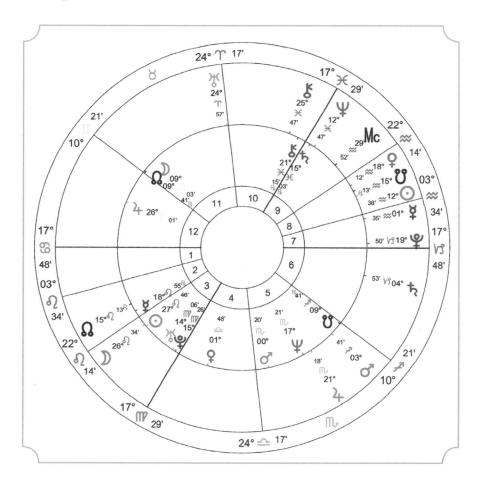

A chart that shows the movement of the planets in relation to their positions at birth.

Erecting a Birth Chart

When I started taking an interest in astrology way back in the 1960s, the only way to make up a chart was by hand, and when I taught astrology, the first four or five lessons always focused on chart calculation. However, even the major astrology schools have long since given up teaching hand calculations as everyone uses software of one kind or another.

An Astrology Website

A site worth trying is astrotheme.com and yet another is cafeastrology.com. There are probably dozens of others available these days.

Your Own App

You can choose from dozens of apps that work on a smartphone or a tablet, and prices range from free to a small sum. At this stage of the game, almost any of these will give you the data that you want.

Software

The range of quality software and the price differentials are dazzling, but a good price for a decent setup is around $100 (£70). If you progress to becoming a professional astrologer, or if you decide to study unusual astrological concepts, you might choose to pay as much as $300 (£200) for a massive program.

By Hand

There are some old-time astrologers who can just about remember how to erect a chart by hand, but these are few and far between. Nowadays, not even the major astrology schools teach chart calculation.

Enclosed Astrology Wall Chart

Included in this book is a wall chart that serves as a quick and handy go-to reference guide containing the major components of astrology summarized from the following pages.

The Concepts

These are the concepts that you will need to learn or to look up in this book in order to give a reading to yourself and to others:

- the twelve signs of the zodiac
- the ascendant or rising sign
- the twelve astrological houses
- the planets
- the aspects
- simple predictive techniques

Once you grasp the nature of the twelve signs of the zodiac, you will have much of this subject under your belt, because the twelve astrological signs link with the twelve houses and the planets also link with the signs and houses. For instance, the sign of Aries, the first house, and Mars share the same characteristics, while the sign of Taurus, the second house, and Venus also share their characteristics, and so on round the zodiac. So in essence, once you have learned twelve pieces of information, the rest will fall into place. After this, there is the matter of putting these pieces of information together in the necessary order, as shown in the birth chart.

A birth chart, or natal chart, is a stylized map of the sky at the time of birth. The birth chart does seem complicated to a beginner, but once you start to work through your own chart, the mists soon start to clear.

The Ecliptic, or Zodiac

The main thing as far as astrologers are concerned is that everything in astrology happens on or near the ecliptic. Consider the sky as a whole for a moment: it's full of stars and many of the constellations are well known—for example, the Big Dipper, the Great Bear, Orion the Hunter, and so on—but none of those count in astrology unless they are on the ecliptic. This is a blessing for us, because it means that we can happily ignore around 99 percent of everything in the sky!

We all know that the earth orbits the sun, but to the ancient astrologers, it looked as if the sun, moon, planets, and stars all orbited the earth. We know this isn't so, but astrologers and astronomers still use the path that the sun appears to take around the earth to navigate our way around the sky. The full name for this trajectory is the *plane of the ecliptic*, but it is usually called the *ecliptic*. However, it is also far better known as the *zodiac*.

The word *zodiac* comes from ancient Greek, and it is from the same root as zoo or zoological gardens, with the "zo" part meaning "a collection of animals." The view from earth shows twelve constellations of stars that lie along the ecliptic, and these form the signs of the zodiac. Ancient astrologers believed these constellations resembled animals or figures that were gods in their day, and they gave them names that fitted their mythology. The gods are long forgotten but their names linger on.

The Glyphs (Symbols)

The word *glyph* means "symbol," rather like the word *hieroglyph*. You are probably used to seeing the glyphs for the signs, but now you will need to learn which is which and get used to writing them down.

Sign	Aries	Taurus	Gemini
Glyph	♈	♉	♊
Sign	Cancer	Leo	Virgo
Glyph	♋	♌	♍
Sign	Libra	Scorpio	Sagittarius
Glyph	♎	♏	♐
Sign	Capricorn	Aquarius	Pisces
Glyph	♑	♒	♓

The Zodiac Symbols

The symbols that we use for the signs of the zodiac were once considered to be actual gods who lived among the stars. Some of these have changed their names over the millennia. For instance, Aries was once ruled by a goose, and Aries has also been called a sheep or goat at some time in the past, while Capricorn was once ruled by a crocodile and Scorpio by an eagle.

Here are the ancient symbols of the signs of the zodiac as we know them today:

Sign	Aries *The Ram*	Taurus *The Bull*	Gemini *The Twins*
Symbol			
Sign	Cancer *The Crab*	Leo *The Lion*	Virgo *The Virgin or Maiden*
Symbol			
Sign	Libra *The Scales*	Scorpio *The Scorpion*	Sagittarius *The Archer or Centaur*
Symbol			
Sign	Capricorn *The Goat*	Aquarius *The Water Carrier*	Pisces *The Fishes*
Symbol			

The Planetary Glyphs

Soon you will also need to get used to recognizing the glyphs for the planets:

Planet	The sun	The moon	Mercury
Glyph	☉	☽	☿
Planet	Venus	Mars	Jupiter
Glyph	♀	♂	♃
Planet	Saturn	Uranus	Neptune
Glyph	♄	♅	♆
Planet	Pluto	Chiron	
Glyph	♇	⚷	

It's obvious that the sun and moon are not planets as the sun is a star and the moon a satellite of the earth, but we call them planets for the sake of simplicity. Incidentally, astronomers have now demoted Pluto to dwarf planet but we still call it a planet in astrology. Another dwarf planet that astrologers have become accustomed to using for the past half century is Chiron.

The Zodiac

If you hated mathematics or geometry when you were at school, don't let the following put you off, because it is easy to understand.

A circle contains 360 degrees and when we split into twelve, each division contains 30 degrees. Each of these divisions is measured from 0° to 29°, and each of these is a sign of the zodiac.

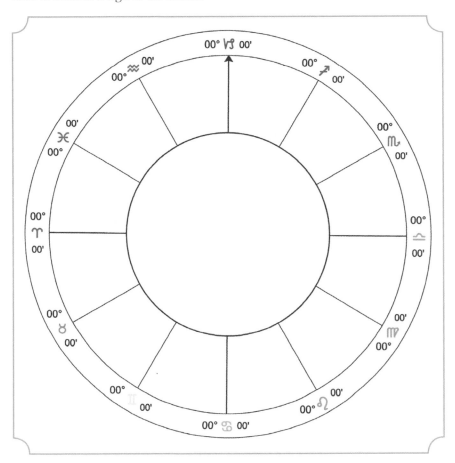

The Zodiac

The Rising Sign and the Ascendant

There are some similarities between a birth chart and a clock or a compass, but the starting point on a birth chart is the ascendant, which is at the nine o'clock position, which is on the left-hand side of the chart. The rising sign is the sign that was rising over the horizon at the time of birth, and the ascendant is *the exact point* within that sign that is rising over the horizon. For instance, on Leonardo DiCaprio's chart, you will see that the ascendant is three degrees and

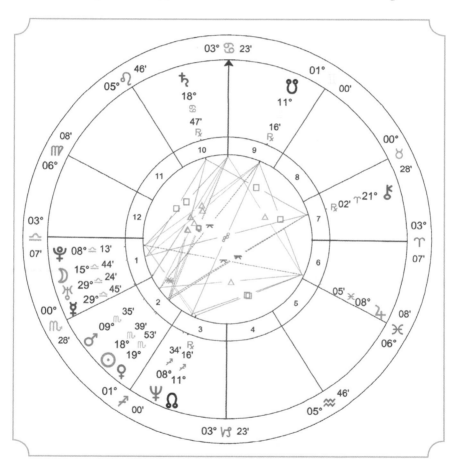

Leonardo DiCaprio's Birth Chart, Showing the Ascendant

seven minutes of Libra, so Leonardo has Libra rising. The houses run round the chart in a counterclockwise direction from the ascendant.

The Astrological Houses

The houses run from one to twelve, and they start from the ascendant and run round the chart in a counterclockwise direction.

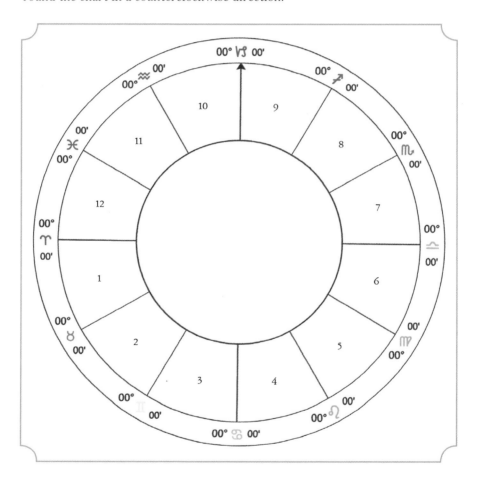

The Houses

The Aspects

The zodiac is a circle, so when the planets are ranged round it, some will be close to each other and others will be at a distance. The distance might be two, three, four, five, or six signs apart, and these distances form the aspects, each of which has a bearing. This is a little advanced for an absolute beginner, so perhaps leave this topic for the time being and come back to it when you have learned the basics.

Predictive Astrology

The natal chart, or birth chart, is a map of the sky at the time of birth, but the earth, the solar system, and everything else move on sooner or later. It is the movement of the planets in juxtaposition with the natal chart that allows us to see what's happening at any one time, to judge what happened in the past, and to predict what will happen in the future. This isn't as hard as it sounds, and you will see the techniques in action toward the end of this book.

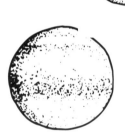

And that just about covers it. There are many other fields of astrology that people like to research and try out, and it would take more than one lifetime to understand them all, but the basics are enough for most people. These are even enough for those who intend to make their living by giving readings to clients or by writing astrology columns in newspapers and magazines.

If you look at Neil Diamond's chart, you will see the signs of the zodiac ranged round the outside, and the planets and other features including the houses and with the innermost part of the chart taken up by lines that represent the aspects.

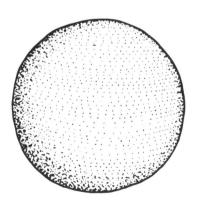

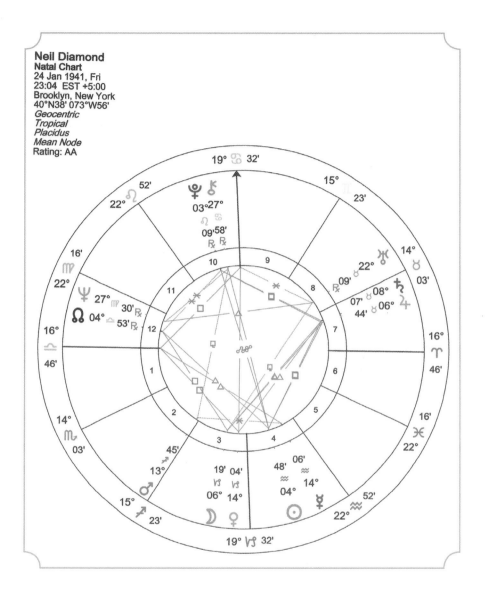

Neil Diamond
Natal Chart
24 Jan 1941, Fri
23:04 EST +5:00
Brooklyn, New York
40°N38' 073°W56'
Geocentric
Tropical
Placidus
Mean Node
Rating: AA

2

THE SIGNS OF THE ZODIAC

The Sun Signs

There are twelve signs of the zodiac, and astrologers often refer to these as *sun signs*. This is because from our position on earth, the sun appears to enter these signs at regular times each year. For instance, at the start of each year, the sun is always in Capricorn, and it moves to the next sign, which is Aquarius, on around January 20th and so on around the system.

The sun doesn't always move out of one sign and into another on exactly the same day each year, so if you were born on the cusp of two signs, you will need to look up your sun sign on an astrology app or enlist the help of an astrologer. This will take only a moment to do, and it is unlikely that an astrologer would ask for money for this service. Meanwhile, here are the *average* dates for the sun signs:

Sign	Dates
Aries ♈	March 21–April 19
Taurus ♉	April 20–May 20
Gemini ♊	May 21–June 21
Cancer ♋	June 22–July 22
Leo ♌	July 23–August 22
Virgo ♍	August 23–September 22
Libra ♎	September 23–October 23
Scorpio ♏	October 24–November 22
Sagittarius ♐	November 23–December 22
Capricorn ♑	December 23–January 20
Aquarius ♒	January 21–February 19
Pisces ♓	February 20–March 20

The Nature of the Signs

There are various ways in which the signs are organized, although some of these categories are more effective than others.

THE GENDERS

Each sign is given a gender, the concept of which is similar to that of yang and yin in the Chinese tradition, because every alternate sign is considered to be either masculine or feminine.

Sign	Aries	Taurus	Gemini
Gender	♂	♀	♂
Sign	Cancer	Leo	Virgo
Gender	♀	♂	♀
Sign	Libra	Scorpio	Sagittarius
Gender	♂	♀	♂
Sign	Capricorn	Aquarius	Pisces
Gender	♀	♂	♀

KEY	Masculine ♂
	Feminine ♀

The Air of Aquarius

Beginners often think Aquarius is a water sign due to its symbol of the Water Carrier, but it is actually an air sign.

THE ELEMENTS

The elements are much more influential than the genders, so they are worth taking on board. Each sign of the zodiac belongs to an element, and these are fire, earth, air, and water. Here is a quick guide to the nature of the elements:

- Fire sign people get things off the ground quickly.
- Earth signs do things in a slow and considered manner.
- Air signs like to talk and analyze.
- Water signs act according to their feelings at any given moment.

Sign	Element
Aries ♈	Fire △
Taurus ♉	Earth ▽
Gemini ♊	Air △
Cancer ♋	Water ▽
Leo ♌	Fire △
Virgo ♍	Earth ▽
Libra ♎	Air △
Scorpio ♏	Water ▽
Sagittarius ♐	Fire △
Capricorn ♑	Earth ▽
Aquarius ♒	Air △
Pisces ♓	Water ▽

THE ELEMENTS

FIRE

Fire sign people are courageous and won't hesitate to plunge headlong into everything life has to offer. Unfortunately, these folk can't always understand why the other zodiac types lack their ability to grasp an opportunity when it arises. Fire people are quick, intelligent, and generous. They love deeply and with passion. They are more sensitive than they appear on the outside, so they can be cut to the quick when the affection and generosity that they unstintingly give others isn't returned.

EARTH

Earth sign people are practical, hardworking, and happiest when doing something useful. They can be relied upon to get a job done, even though it might take them a while to get around to doing things. These folk are sensual and have a creative streak, although this manifests itself in different ways with each of the three earth signs. Shrewd and cautious, these people need material and emotional security, but they will put up with a lot for their families.

AIR

If an idea is needed, the air sign person can come up with the answer, but don't count on them to do something they don't understand. Air people are excellent communicators who work in fields where they liaise with others or create connections between groups of people. Many enjoy working with modern technology. They are restless and often tense, and they need travel and a sporty outlet or a practical hobby, such as gardening. Despite being restless and flirtatious, they enjoy being in a loving relationship.

WATER

These people's feelings run deeply, and they can be very emotional. Their loved ones will discover what it is like to live alongside their spells of excitement and joy and their times of depression. These people approach matters in an indirect manner, testing out a situation before plunging in. They are, however, intuitive, so they feel everything that is going on in the atmosphere around them. Water people attach themselves strongly to those they love, and they are especially close to their children. Most are also fond of pets.

THE QUALITIES

There are three qualities—cardinal, fixed, and mutable—and these are another very important personality factor. This is a quick guide to the nature of the qualities:

- Cardinal sign people like their own way; they are hard to push around and influence. They make changes when a situation no longer suits them.
- Fixed sign people uphold the status quo and don't change direction easily.
- Mutable sign people are adaptable. They work in jobs where they travel around or deal with a flow of different people or goods during the course of each day.

Sign	Quality
Aries ♈	Cardinal
Taurus ♉	Fixed
Gemini ♊	Mutable
Cancer ♋	Cardinal
Leo ♌	Fixed
Virgo ♍	Mutable
Libra ♎	Cardinal
Scorpio ♏	Fixed
Sagittarius ♐	Mutable
Capricorn ♑	Cardinal
Aquarius ♒	Fixed
Pisces ♓	Mutable

Putting It All Together

If you look carefully at the table, you will see that each sign has its own individual combination of factors. It will share its gender with five others, its element with two others, and its quality with three others, but its own combination is unique:

Sign	Gender	Element	Quality
Aries ♈	♂	Fire △	Cardinal
Taurus ♉	♀	Earth ▽	Fixed
Gemini ♊	♂	Air △	Mutable
Cancer ♋	♀	Water ▽	Cardinal
Leo ♌	♂	Fire △	Fixed
Virgo ♍	♀	Earth ▽	Mutable
Libra ♎	♂	Air △	Cardinal
Scorpio ♏	♀	Water ▽	Fixed
Sagittarius ♐	♂	Fire △	Mutable
Capricorn ♑	♀	Earth ▽	Cardinal
Aquarius ♒	♂	Air △	Fixed
Pisces ♓	♀	Water ▽	Mutable

3

THE SUN
SIGNS

Aries

March 21–April 19

Planet: Mars
Symbol: The Ram
Gender: Masculine
Element: Fire
Quality: Cardinal

Aries is the first sign of the zodiac. It is associated with the start of the ancient Roman year and the start of spring. It is a masculine fire sign, which means that Arians move quickly when they want to. It is also a cardinal sign, which makes them hard to influence or push around. Arians can get anything they want off the ground, but their schemes may backfire. They are quick to think and to act, are often intelligent, and have no patience for fools or those who they consider slower than themselves.

Arians are courageous, ambitious, and keen to take risks in order to attain their goals. Some are so dynamic that they unnerve others, although this is more likely to be expressed in the area of work than in their private lives. Arians can stay in the same job for years, but they prefer to make progress in a job that they feel is meaningful and useful to society. Many work in large organizations, such as schools, hospitals, the armed forces or law enforcement. Where home life is concerned, most Arians love and respect their families and prefer to stay in a relationship for years without straying, although there are some who find it hard to settle down with one person.

Aries people love their homes and will try to hang on to them even in tough times. They like to choose the way the home is arranged and decorated, and they may try to impose their wills on their partners about such things. Arians value loyalty, so they need their partners to be faithful and to help them cope with their occasional lapses of self-confidence. Their faults are those of impatience and impetuosity, coupled with a hot temper. Aries people can be foolish over money matters and they can be wasteful. Some buy far more clothes than they can possibly wear and then forget to look after them properly, while others don't look after their homes properly. Some love fast cars and will spend money on these before other considerations. The worst Aries traits are selfishness and a lack of common sense. They are not always the tidiest of people, and they are impatient with details, except when engaged in their specialist subjects.

> ### Common Aries Attributes
>
> ••••◆◆◆◆◆••••
>
> In European races, many Arians have fair or red hair.

Their best traits are courage, fortitude, intelligence, loyalty, and humor. Arians are sociable, neighborly, and generous, and their idealism often leads them into politics or some form of work that benefits society as a whole. They have kind hearts and can be generous and helpful toward others. They are idealistic and will fight for the rights of others, which is why so many Arians get involved in local or national politics.

Aries people will sacrifice a great deal to ensure that their children have all that they need, and they see education as the key to success. Never being one to grumble and moan, they get better in old age, because they keep on going and retain their sense of humor as time goes by. They are faithful while in love but if love begins to fade, they start to look around. Many Arians are artistic, especially when it comes to technical drawing, while others make wonderful mechanics and engineers. Many are excellent software designers, and they can be real innovators in these fields.

Taurus

April 20–May 20

Planet: Venus
Symbol: The Bull
Gender: Feminine
Element: Earth
Quality: Fixed

Taurus is a feminine earth sign, and Taureans are thorough, sensible, and capable. They can achieve a good deal, as long as they are allowed to do so at their own pace. This is a fixed sign, and the combination of earth and fixity means that this is the most obstinate sign of the zodiac. Taurus people are loyal, dependable, unchanging, and stable, which makes it hard for them to cope when a little adaptability is needed. These people are practical and persevering, solid and reliable.

Their love of money and the comfort it brings may make them materialistic in outlook. They are most suited to a practical career that brings few surprises but which earns them a decent income. They also have a strong artistic streak, which can be expressed in their work, hobbies, and interests.

Taureans are sociable, so they make friends easily, and love to be out and about with their pals. Their humor and sociability make them a welcome addition to any party or event, while their interests are wide ranging and their knowledge of their specialist subjects is deep.

Taurus people fear poverty and they have a strong sense of responsibility, so they will always look for a steady job that offers a regular income for themselves and their families. While some are ambitious, many are satisfied with a safe and comfortable position in the middle lane. Taureans can spend quite freely on travel or hobbies, but they won't waste money or spend unnecessarily when times are hard. Family life is dear to these people, and they are generous when it comes to the needs of their loved ones. Taureans usually make good family members and they care deeply about their loved ones, but their obstinacy means that they can dig their heels in when it isn't really necessary. Some make good counselors as they aren't particularly judgmental about the failings of others.

> ## Common Taurus Attributes
>
> ·····◆◆◆◆◆◆◆·····
>
> Many Taureans are graceful and good looking. Many are good singers and dancers.

Many Taureans develop bees in their bonnets about some subject that interests them, and they can make themselves boring if this is carried to excess, but most have enough common sense to prevent this from happening. All have a keen sense of beauty, while many are artistic and creative. The fields of fashion, décor, makeup, and hairstyling appeal to this sign, and this leads many into the sidelines of the fashion trade or show business. This sign is associated with the voice and with music, so these people often like to sing, and many join choirs or play and sing in pop or country groups for the sheer pleasure of it. Some work in hypnotherapy, where the quiet and gentle voice becomes an important part of their job. Many are good cooks.

These people are courageous and their virtues are common sense, loyalty, responsibility, and a pleasant approach to others. Taureans are much brighter than anyone gives them credit for, and it is hard to best them in an argument because they usually know what they are talking about. When a Taurean is on your side, they make wonderful friends and reliable colleagues.

Gemini

May 21–June 21
Planet: Mercury
Symbol: The Twins
Gender: Masculine
Element: Air
Quality: Mutable

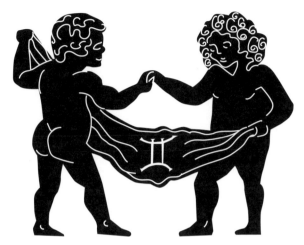

This is an air sign, so Gemini people have active minds and they are intelligent. The connection with the Roman god Mercury, who was the messenger of the gods, makes them good communicators, and they are certainly friendly and sociable. The mutable aspect of the sign makes Geminis adaptable. Many Geminis have a good head for figures, which leads them into careers in banking, accountancy, and statistical work. These people are quick on the uptake and are great thinkers and planners; as this is the sign of the mentality rather than of the emotions, their minds are never still for long. They can be tough negotiators and clever businesspeople, but they have to guard against impulsiveness or, in some cases, a tendency to bully those who aren't in a position to stand up to them.

Geminis are often accused of being unable to stick to anything for long and of having superficial knowledge of many subjects rather than knowing one subject well, but this is unfair as Geminis are very determined when there is something that they set their minds on, and they study deeply when something interests them. They can be very hard workers who put a great deal of effort into what they do, and they don't watch the clock. Many are worriers, and it is easy for them to get wound up over things that others wouldn't think twice about. They can feel very insecure in their careers or personal life even when things are going well, so they need more reassurance than outsiders realize. Some Geminis are deprived of security, love, or attention in childhood, while others lack material goods during their childhood. They eventually solve these problems by earning good money and by finding the right person to love—

although it sometimes takes them time to find the right person.

The downside of this sign is that their sharp tongues can break up a perfectly viable relationship. Some Geminis are too fond of drink, while others are spendthrifts when it comes to clothes and accessories, and as they rarely part with anything they buy, their closets soon become stuffed.

> ## Common Gemini Attributes
>
> ·····◆◆◆◆◆◆·····
>
> Many Geminis are talkative and they use their hands when explaining things.

Geminis want to make their relationships last, but if a partnership fails, they will soon start looking for the next. They will do all they can to ensure their family has everything it needs and that their children have a good education and a good start in life. They read and learn throughout life and have a wide area of knowledge. They are often immensely talented. They are kindhearted and will help friends, neighbors, and acquaintances, but they don't have deep wells of emotional strength, so they can't put up with lame ducks for long. Their friendly attitude and excellent communications skills ensure that they have a great social life; they are ready to go anywhere at the drop of a hat and are good fun to be with. Gemini is a mutable sign, so Geminis usually get around a lot in their jobs and deal with a variety of people, goods, services, and ideas during the course of each day.

Cancer

June 22–July 22

Planet: The moon
Symbol: The Crab
Gender: Feminine
Element: Water
Quality: Cardinal

Cancer is ruled by the moon, which makes this sign sensitive and emotional. It is a feminine sign and a water sign, both of which add intuition, a caring nature, and a desire to help others and to protect their family. The other side of the coin is that this is a cardinal sign, and therefore hard to influence, and these people are much tougher than others realize.

Cancerians are shy when young, and although they overcome this problem to a great extent when older, many dislike being in the limelight. This sign has a reputation for being home-loving, but while Cancerians definitely need a base and a home to call their own, they enjoy getting out of the house and traveling. Indeed, many take jobs that involve moving around and meeting different people during the course of their day.

Cancerians tend to grow up quickly and some take on family responsibilities when still young, possibly due to being the oldest child in a large family. They continue to take a responsible attitude to their loved ones once they reach adulthood, and they retain plenty of family contact throughout life. They can have intense relationships with their mothers, so they either remain extremely close to their mothers or fall out badly with them at some point. For the most part, though, they care deeply for their children and loved ones. They are good cooks and make comfortable homes for their loved ones to occupy, while also being shrewd and having good heads for business.

Cancerians find it easy to tap into the needs of the public, so they often choose careers that involve dealing with the public, especially shop work or perhaps running restaurants. Cancer people often choose to work in sales, particularly in things that are used around the home, while others work in finance, real estate, or insurance, all of which help people to buy and insure their homes.

> **Common Cancer Attributes**
>
> Many Cancerians are gentle looking and sometimes slow to react when called upon.

Many Cancerians work in teaching or the caring professions. They have a feel for history and may collect historical mementos. Their memory is excellent. Many are excellent listeners and have an uncanny knack of defusing difficult situations, all of which makes them good counselors. They can put up with any amount of noise, chaos, and arguments at work, but they need peace and tranquility at home. Where their own problems are concerned, they can disappear inside themselves and brood, which makes them hard for others to understand. Cancerians spend a good deal of time worrying about their families and sometimes about money, and while they appear soft, they are actually very hard to influence. They can also be lazy and apt to want others to provide for them.

Cancerians won't stay with a partner who treats them badly, but they do tend to keep in touch with family members, even after a split, as long as the situation isn't too acrimonious. One major downside of this sign is a tendency to be hurtful to those who they perceive to be weak, and some can behave very badly toward sons-in-law and daughters-in-law. Some have strange attitudes to money. Others are moody and possessive, which makes them exhausting to live with. Fortunately, most have common sense and a reasonable attitude to others and to financial matters. However, their changeability and tendency to take decisions from an emotional standpoint can cause problems for themselves as well as for others.

Leo

July 23–August 22

Planet: The sun
Symbol: The Lion
Gender: Masculine
Element: Fire
Quality: Fixed

This is a masculine fire sign so these people get jobs done quickly when the need arises, but Leos are also logical and organized. Being a fixed sign, Leos don't chop and change direction, and they will do all they can to uphold the status quo.

Leos are so capable that they are easily irritated by those who don't do things as quickly and efficiently as they themselves do, and they can't understand people who allow opportunities to pass them by. Sometimes it is early struggles in life that make Leos so ambitious and self-reliant. Many are attracted to glamorous professions such as the airline or entertainment industry, banking, publishing, or the travel trade, and they soon become involved in the business or administrative sides of these careers. Many run small businesses of their own, because they enjoy running their own show. Leos love music and many play an instrument or sing and dance, and some even take to a life on the stage. They aren't fazed by being out there in front of an audience. Others spend their day communing with computers and other high-tech gadgetry.

There are people of this sign who are *not* glamorous, charismatic, or successful in worldly terms, but these people put their considerable energies into ensuring that their children go as far as they possibly can in life. Leos tend to marry and produce a family when they are still young, and their children quickly become the light of their lives. These affectionate people make loving partners and wonderful parents, although they don't allow their children to get away with bad behavior. Leos value honesty, decency, loyalty, and generosity,

and while some can
be arrogant and
unpleasant, most have
a good moral compass.

Leos may look
grand, and may want to
be in charge and to be
treated like royalty, but
in reality they are great

Common Leo Attributes

Many Leos are good dancers and many worry about their hair—especially Leo men!

big softies who love to give and receive affection. Under normal circumstances, they are warmhearted, generous, sociable, and popular, but they can be very moody and irritable when under pressure or when feeling unwell. Leos put their heart and soul into whatever they are doing and they can work like demons, but they cannot keep up the pace for long and need to stretch out on the sofa and rest when fatigue sets in. They also need frequent holidays in order to recharge their batteries. These people always appear confident and they look like true winners, but their confidence can suddenly evaporate, leaving them unsure and unhappy with their efforts. They are extremely sensitive and cannot take ridicule or even much teasing. Most are good homemakers and great cooks, but they love eating out and socializing with others over a nice meal and a good glass of wine.

Some spend money on luxuries that they can't afford, or they spend money on their family when they can't really afford to do so. They love the status and lifestyle that proclaim their successes. Leos are proud, and have very high standards in all that they do, and most of them have great integrity and honesty. Leos can stand on their dignity and be very snobbish. Leo faults are bossiness and short temper, and their arrogance can become insufferable.

In loving relationships, Leos are loyal and will go the extra mile for their partners. The fixed nature of this sign means they prefer to stay with the same partner for life, but they can start looking around if the partner doesn't appreciate or love them. They are also able to bear a grudge.

Virgo

August 23–September 22

Planet: Mercury
Symbol: The Virgin, or Maiden
Gender: Feminine
Element: Earth
Quality: Mutable

Virgos are some of the hardest workers of the zodiac and they have the patience to cope with detailed work, but they have delicate nervous systems and can get sick if put under too much pressure. Many are drawn to the fields of health and healing, and while some work in the established medical field, others may take up alternative healing.

The Virgo childhood is likely to have been difficult, with parents or schoolteachers who perhaps were unnecessarily harsh or critical toward them. It is possible that the Virgo child came into the lives of the parents at an awkward time, or that having a child changed the parents' lifestyles in a way that they didn't like, all of which can lead to frustration that spills over onto the child. Early unhappiness can lead Virgos to leave home when they are young, possibly by moving in with a lover or by getting married. Once they do this, they try to make the relationship work, but it can fall apart quickly due to youth, lack of money, and lack of life experience.

Some find other ways of jumping into adulthood early, perhaps by joining the armed forces or doing charity work overseas or even by going onto the stage. The last idea isn't as far fetched as it might seem, because many Virgos are good actors and broadcasters, and many do well in the field of entertainment. Those who get a good education may find work in a field of communication, and there are many working in the world of publishing, in books or in other media. Some Virgos have good singing voices, and most listen to a lot of music. Being an earth sign, there is a powerful emotional side to this person, which leads to the Virgo losing himself in music or enjoying a good book.

> ## Common Virgo Attributes
>
> ••••••••••••
>
> Many Virgos are slim and good looking, and they keep their looks for longer than most.

Virgos take their responsibilities seriously, and once they do settle into a permanent relationship, their families can rely on them for support, but they may become so caught up in work that they neglect their partner and children. If Virgos find themselves with a partner who proves to be difficult, demanding, pushy, or wearing, they just don't have the emotional strength to live in a battleground, so will leave the relationship. They are fond of small animals, and often have much-loved cats, dogs, rabbits, and so on, and they never abandon any of these creatures.

These people have an academic turn of mind, but this doesn't prevent them from having fun, enjoying holidays, and taking time off for things that interest them. Their sense of humor and absolute reliability, along with their kind hearts, make them wonderful friends, while their ability to listen and empathize makes them excellent counselors. The weird thing is that, despite the fact that they have very good, and very quick, minds, they aren't great when pushed into things suddenly. Earth signs are always better when they have time to think things through and do them at their own pace; if they rush to judgment, they make mistakes.

Virgo can be neurotic worriers and can take this tendency to neuroticism to extreme lengths, which is irritating and boring to others. They are perfectionists who can be critical of others, although they are often equally critical of themselves. Although ambitious, when faced with potential success, they can also shoot themselves in the foot and spoil their own chances.

Libra

September 23–October 23

Planet: Venus
Symbol: The Scales
Gender: Masculine
Element: Air
Quality: Cardinal

From a technical point of view, Libra is a confusing sign. For one thing, this is the only sign symbolized by an inanimate object; second, it is a masculine sign ruled by Venus, which is a very feminine planet. It belongs to the element of air, which is cool, detached, and logical rather than emotional, but this is offset by the go-getting focused cardinal quality. With this strange passive/aggressive mixture, is it any wonder that Librans are so indecisive?

Librans are masters of tact and diplomacy and good friends to all who come into contact with them. However, there is a strange element of detachment and self-absorption that can make it hard for others to ever feel really close to them. Some Librans spend their lives looking for the ideal partner; others are so independent that after trying a few relationships, they settle for their own company and for doing things in their own way. Librans are also flirtatious, which is flattering and enjoyable as long as nobody takes their flirting too seriously.

Their pleasing personalities and smooth charm take refined Librans into jobs where their manners are appreciated. They make sympathetic dentists, lawyers, and accountants whose client base grows, as much through their ability to put people at ease as through their undoubted talent. Their love of bringing people together and of smoothing over problems takes them into agency work, arbitration, negotiating, and business. Being intelligent and good with their hands, they can go into dress designing or engineering, but they can also be drawn to the beauty industry.

Common Libra Attributes

•••◆◆◆◆◆◆•••

Many Librans tip their heads to one side and sit or stand with one shoulder higher than the other.

Many Librans can be found in the world of music, and they also make excellent dancers. Another world that attracts this sign is the law. The desire to bring a settlement between groups of people along with an intense hatred of injustice makes them capable lawyers.

One thing for certain is that most Librans will go into a field where they can earn good money, because they need a high standard of living. They are generous to their loved ones, so they are happy to keep a partner in comfort, although they do appreciate it if their partner has a job. Both sexes enjoy domestic activities and many are excellent cooks—and some love to grow the food they cook.

This is a cardinal sign, which makes it hard for Librans to compromise, so while they may talk about agreements, shared interests, and cooperation, there is a strict limit to the amount of compromise they are willing to bring to bear. And yet they dislike their own company and somehow manage to have partners, friends, and colleagues aplenty, although they probably "do" friendship better than close relationships. Librans can be wonderful company, but when in the wrong mood, they can be argumentative and deeply unpleasant, and they don't hold back from saying what they feel or hurting others for the sake of it. This is a truly confusing sign, with so much that is good and so much that is hard to stomach.

Scorpio

October 24–November 22

Planet: Pluto
Symbol: The Scorpion
Gender: Feminine
Element: Water
Quality: Fixed

This is a fairly confusing sign, as it is a feminine water sign, which one would consider to be weak and gentle, but Scorpios are far from weak and not all of them are gentle. The watery nature of the sign means that Scorpios make decisions based on the way they feel at any specific time. They also believe (or profess to believe) in one set of rules on one day and a completely different set on the next day. They are extremely sensitive and prone to being hurt and upset, so they go to great lengths to hide their vulnerable side and to keep others from hurting them.

This is a passionate all-or-nothing sign, and these people can take things to the limit. For instance, Scorpios can be very abstemious *or* heavy drinkers; they can be thrifty and frugal *or* absolute spendthrifts; they can be generous in some ways and selfish in others. Some are kind and helpful and others aren't, or they can change from one thing to the other according to their mood. Nobody is more charming and hospitable when they want company, but they can be difficult when they don't.

Scorpios are very persuasive, which makes them excellent salespeople or counselors, but this can tip over into manipulative behavior or even a subtle form of bullying. Many are drawn to work in the areas of health and healing, which may take them into the established medical field or into some kind of alternative or complementary therapy, and they can be excellent psychic healers. This sign has a powerful sense of intuition and it sees through people, so this makes Scorpios excellent detectives, investigators, and lawyers. Some find their way into the armed forces. These people take their work seriously and often work very hard,

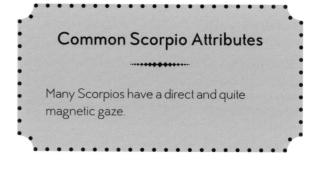

Common Scorpio Attributes

Many Scorpios have a direct and quite magnetic gaze.

possibly because they seek the respect and approval of others. Scorpios enjoy being the power behind the throne with someone else occupying the hot seat, which is partly due to a lack of confidence. Many people of this sign work in finance and banking, often in a capacity where they advise others on how to handle mortgages, loans, overdrafts, insurance, pension schemes, and so on. Others are solicitors who specialize in wills and trust funds.

Scorpios' voices are their best feature, as these are often low, well-modulated, and cultured, and they use them well when in the mood to persuade others. These people are neither as highly sexed or as difficult as most astrology books make them out to be, but they do have their passions (even if these are not always for sex itself) and they like to be thought of as sexy. They love to shock and can enjoy teasing others, but they also make kindhearted and loyal friends and great hosts.

Some Scorpios love animals and are very good with them, while others are wonderful with small children and love nothing better than to play with them. Most enjoy family life, especially when children and grandchildren come along.

Sagittarius

November 23–December 22

Planet: Jupiter
Symbol: The Archer, or Centaur
Gender: Masculine
Element: Fire
Quality: Mutable

Sagittarius is a masculine fire sign, so these people think and act quickly. They can see the overall picture but may have difficulty in handling details. Being a mutable sign, these subjects are adaptable and able to fit into a new environment more easily than most. This is a good thing on the whole, because people of this sign are apt to move from one area to another or even one country to another at various times throughout their lives.

Sagittarians come in two distinct packages. Some are quiet, shy, short of confidence, and really happy only when with family or close friends, whereas others are among the most outgoing people in the zodiac. These folk are hard workers who can be quite successful in a career, but occasional lapses of confidence or foolish decisions can trip them up or prevent them from reaching their full potential. Sagittarius is known as a lucky sign, so these people manage to fall on their feet even in the toughest of times. Many are drawn to astrology and mystical arts and most have a philosophical turn of mind, but they often turn away from the religion of their parents or educators. They may appear superficial to outsiders, but the truth is that they think deeply and can be studious.

Sagittarians are active, so they dislike sitting around for long. They love to be on the move and dislike being tied to one place, especially where their work is concerned. Most choose jobs where they meet a variety of different people. Sometimes the job takes them from place to place, or they may have hobbies or interests that encourage them to get out and about. Despite an appearance of great energy, like all fire signs, Sagittarians tire easily and need time to give their bodies and nerves a rest.

Jobs can range from vicar and teacher to tradesman, electrician, joiner, travel agent, bus or taxi driver, tailor, shop worker, or anything else that deals with a host of people during the course of

Common Sagittarius Attributes

Many Sagittarians have a lovely smile.

a workweek. Veterinary work or even something odd such as training predator hawks— or training new recruits to the air force—might appeal to them. Many Sagittarians work as astrologers, psychics, Tarot readers, and palmists. Sagittarians of both sexes are extremely clever with their hands, so building and refurbishing a home is something that they find easy. They also love being outdoors, so they travel the country and explore their surroundings, and when young, they enjoy active holidays in fun-filled locations. Most enjoy keeping pets.

A partner who nags or makes unreasonable demands will soon get these individuals down, as would a partner who restricts the Sagittarian's movements. These people hate an injustice, but their honesty can make them a little tactless and apt to upset others, albeit unwittingly. There is a side to them that never quite grows up, which ensures that they are truly fun-loving partners or parents. Sometimes a bad childhood can make this sign sad and lonely, so they need a supportive and loving partner.

Capricorn

December 23–January 20

Planet: Saturn
Symbol: The Goat
Gender: Feminine
Element: Earth
Quality: Cardinal

Capricorn is a feminine earth sign, which denotes practicality, common sense, and attention to details. It is also a cardinal sign, which means these people can't be pushed around or made to do things they don't want to do. They don't rush into things, but they have a tendency to get what they want in the long run. When Capricorns set their caps at someone and decide this is the person they want, they will wait half a lifetime if that's what it takes to get the person for themselves. They often choose older partners, and sometimes there is a surprisingly large age gap, but these people often feel more comfortable with people who are older than they are.

All Capricorns are ambitious in one way or another if not for themselves, then for their children. They see to it that their children receive the best education and make the best of their opportunities. Being practical, sensible, realistic, and responsible, Capricorns take life quite seriously, but that doesn't make them humorless or dull—they can have a wonderfully dry sense of humor. Some are happy to remain single, possibly due to shyness and awkwardness with love interests, but perhaps because they end up staying with their parents and looking after them in later life. When they get into a relationship, they take it very seriously indeed and bend heaven and earth to make it work.

Capricorns can be fussy, and can worry over nothing and take offense over nothing, and they can alienate people by their prickly attitude. Some may allow their ambition to sweep them over the edge into dubious practices, but most tread the straight and narrow path. Career choices can lead almost anywhere, but business of any kind attracts them, with accountancy and banking high on the list. Many long to own land, so farming and property development can appeal to them. Traditional astrology suggests that science in all its forms is attached to this sign.

> ## Common Capricorn Attributes
>
> Many Capricorns are slim and good looking with lovely hair.

Sitting between the two most unconventional signs of the zodiac (Sagittarius and Aquarius) can rub off on this sign, so Capricorns may have unusual interests and talents. Many are keen on astrology, palmistry, psychism, and mystical matters, and surprisingly many are good dancers. Some are experts on antiques or knowledgeable stamp collectors, great cooks, or winners at some oddball sport.

Capricorns are patient, realistic, and responsible and they take life seriously, so they need security but may find this difficult to achieve. Many live on a treadmill of work, simply to pay the bills, but their ambition and longing for status makes them climb the ladder of success one way or another. Some marry into class, money, or the power-broker world. When these subjects run their own businesses, they need a partner who can deal with sales and marketing for them while they keep an eye on the books. Their nit-picking habits can infuriate others, and some have a tendency to "know best." Capricorns are faithful and reliable in relationships and it takes a great deal to make them stray, so if a relationship breaks up, they take a long time to get over it.

Aquarius

January 21–February 19
Planet: Uranus
Symbol: The Water Carrier
Gender: Masculine
Element: Air
Quality: Fixed

This is a masculine fixed sign with the element of air. Beginners in astrology often think this is a water sign, due to the symbol of the Water Carrier, but it is definitely an air sign. Air signs are often happier in the world of ideas than of feelings, and Aquarians are never short of ideas but sometimes lack the practicality to put them into action. They can spend more time thinking, researching, or talking about ideas than getting things done. Inventive, clever, and often ingenious, these subjects can find a way around problems more successfully than any other sign of the zodiac. They appear confident, but they can suffer from shyness and a lack of confidence, although very few people are allowed to see this side of them.

People with this kindly and extremely humanitarian sign often work for the betterment of others and can become wrapped up in causes, sometimes taking things to extremes and neglecting their own families. Their chief faults are forgetfulness and not being able to get anywhere on time, due to doing too much at the last minute.

Aquarians love to teach and they have the world of patience for those who are willing to learn. They speak slowly, express themselves clearly, and always put ideas across in a logical, imaginative manner. Many Aquarians work in the caring professions, while many more are fascinated by computers, so if they can find a technical job with a human side to it, they are probably in the right career. These subjects need a family, but they also need to be independent, so a clingy partner or highly demanding children will get them down. A surprisingly large number of Aquarians avoid having children and many prefer the company of animals to children, and even to adults. If their loved ones respect the need to take time out for hobbies or get away from work, life, and the home for a while, they can be very happy. Clever, friendly, kind, and humane, Aquarians

Common Aquarius Attributes

Aquarians can be tall and rawboned or small and round, and they are friendly and approachable.

are the easiest people to make friends with, but probably the hardest to really know. Being dutiful, they would never let a member of their family go without their basic requirements, but they can be strangely, even deliberately, blind to the underlying needs and real feelings of their children or loved ones. They are often more comfortable with causes and idealistic ideas than with the day-to-day routine of family life; in some cases, their homes may reflect this lack of interest by being rather messy with books everywhere.

These people can be extremely unconventional in the way they dress or the way they live, and they make a point of being different. Some are deeply into astrology, numerology, Egyptology, and so on, whereas others appear conventional, even though they may have unconventional hobbies. Their restless, skeptical minds mean that they need an alternative kind of lifestyle, and although their appearance is cool and calm, Aquarians are tense inside and their bottled-up feelings can explode on occasion into irrational behavior. They are extremely loyal and faithful once they find the right partner.

Pisces

February 20–March 20

Planet: Neptune
Symbol: The Fishes
Gender: Feminine
Element: Water
Quality: Mutable

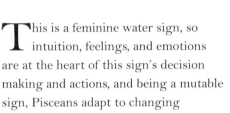

This is a feminine water sign, so intuition, feelings, and emotions are at the heart of this sign's decision making and actions, and being a mutable sign, Pisceans adapt to changing circumstances better than most. These qualities are useful because there is always some kind of chaos going on in their lives, although it may be confined to one area of life; for instance, the person may have everything going well at work, only to find that his domestic life is a mess.

The Piscean's early life is often harsh, with parents who don't think much of him, so Pisceans leave home at an early age to make their own way, getting into partnerships when young— often with other Pisceans. These early relationships may not endure, but many remain friends with their ex-partners and even take care of them when the need arises. Most are very attached to their families and are good to their children and often their grandchildren as well, but their loved ones can take advantage of them. They jump in quickly to help others, often burdening themselves with everyone else's responsibilities. These individuals hate to see others in pain and will rush in to help, but they aren't strong themselves, so they must guard against attracting lame ducks.

Oddly enough, Pisceans can be extremely successful in business, especially when they work in a sales or marketing capacity. They understand the needs of people and their pleasant, nonjudgmental nature means they can put things across in a way that others might envy. They make money by ensuring their company has the right kind of goods and services to offer their customers. They always have a large number of contacts, which are useful when they need to expand their horizons.

Pisces people are creative, which can take them into writing, music, the arts, or the fashion trade, and they love repairing old objects. With values that are spiritual rather than material, these people rarely become rich, but they manage to have what they need. Many Pisceans feel insecure, and most experience poverty at some time in their lives. These individuals are extremely intuitive and many take an interest in spiritualism, clairvoyance, astrology, the Tarot, and so on.

Common Pisces Attributes

Many Pisceans are friendly and approachable, and they have a lovely smile.

Pisceans tend to travel quite a bit during their lifetimes, and they can live in a variety of interesting places or they may have a mobile home or homes in two places at once. They love the sea and many own their own boat. These people can be stubborn, awkward, and nasty when things go sour, but they are rarely vindictive. They prefer to help rather than harm others. Many adore animals, and most have a pet or two to care for, and some will choose to work for the benefit of animals.

The downside of this sign is a tendency to drink too much either socially or when life gets difficult, and many Pisceans get ill as a result of overindulgence. This sign's saving grace is its ability to go with the flow and also to see the humorous side of things, even during the darkest times. They are great company and lovely friends, but they tend to drift out of people's lives when they feel the urge to float away.

✳ ✳ ✳

4

THE RISING SIGN AND THE ASCENDANT

The rising sign occurs at the point where the sun rises over the eastern horizon. The ascendant is the exact point within the rising sign, and it is the starting point for the twelve astrological houses.

The rising sign can be more obvious than the sun sign, so when someone asks you to guess their "star sign" and you get it wrong, it's likely that you are picking up their rising sign rather than the sun sign. The rising sign can modify the person's appearance, manner, and behavior. The rising sign tells us a lot about a person's childhood and youth, and it relates to the kind of programming the individual received while growing up. Nature is within our sun sign and moon sign and the other planets, but nurture can affect our rising sign—sometimes in a big way.

Aries Rising

This subject has a quiet voice and a fairly unobtrusive manner until something irritates him, and then he comes out fighting. He doesn't present a friendly or approachable manner to outsiders because he is quiet and rather remote. His parents may have moved around while he was young, so he grows a tough shell and a belligerent attitude for self-protection. The problem is that he can lash out and attack others without taking

the time to think about the implications, for instance, by attacking those who have no intention of hurting him. He goes after the things he wants without considering the surrounding factors and implications. One or both of his parents may have been unreasonable, so confrontations are likely as he reaches his teens. This person may leave home early, either by taking a job away from home or by marrying young.

He may choose to work in the armed forces, engineering, or especially, the world of construction and property development, but oddly enough, he can find himself among people who are into the psychic sciences or New Age subjects.

The cusp of the second house is in Taurus, so this person will be clever at finding, keeping, and making money. He could be extremely lucky in his work or in his choice of marriage partner, all of which should lead to financial security.

Aries: Put It All Together

This is a masculine, cardinal, fire sign, so there is a strict limit to what this individual will put up with.

Taurus Rising

The childhood home may have been materially comfortable, but it may not have been very happy. Perhaps one of the parents was neurotic or demanding, or schoolteachers or schoolmates made this individual feel inferior in some way. This subject has a good mind, but his attitude may make

him overly sensitive and difficult to work with or live with and he may waste opportunities. He can be good company and a good friend, but he can spoil close relationships by being difficult.

This person is artistic, creative, and clever, so he may work in the field of beauty, the fashion trade, or show business, especially the world of music and singing. He might work as an artist or a designer, a garden designer, or an inspired cook, or he may have hobbies in these fields. He is practical and capable, so he may go into farming, construction, or large-scale enterprises.

Another possibility is banking or big business. This person's main virtue is common sense and his main fault is materialism.

With a second house cusp in Gemini, the Taurus rising person's finances will fluctuate and there will be times when he is well off. He may also save money on some things and overspend on others.

Taurus: Put It All Together

This is a feminine, fixed, earth sign, so this person digs his heels in and won't give way, even when compromise might be better.

Gemini Rising

I call this the sign of the orphan, because even if the person isn't an orphan, he probably feels like it. The family may be dysfunctional or simply unlucky, but whatever the story, the childhood was difficult. The Gemini rising child is bright and remains clever throughout life, but he may have found it hard to fit in at school or with the family and he was never "teacher's pet." It is likely that he achieved very little at school but went on to study and become qualified in something that interested him later in life when his circumstances were more settled.

This person appears amusing, brittle, and possibly even hard, but this image is a shield built up over the decades to hide vulnerability and a kind heart. The image he projects is competent, tough, and businesslike. This person is quick to catch on, and he gets things done.

Being a good communicator, this person might work as a writer or in the media, but he is also likely to have a job that takes him around his neighborhood, such as driving a taxi or a bus. He is good with the public and makes friends

> **Gemini: Put It All Together**
>
> ⋯⋯◆◆◆◆◆◆◆⋯⋯
>
> This is a masculine, mutable, air sign, with no shortage of bright ideas, but this person is happiest when supported by a loving partner.

easily, so he might work in a shop or store. Some go into jobs that involve advising others, with accountancy being a common choice. He might be a good mechanic, but teaching is another option, or coaching children in a sport.

With the second house cusp, this apparently light and insubstantial person is surprisingly shrewd where it comes to money. He may never become rich, but he will manage his money well.

Cancer Rising

There is always a powerful attachment to the mother with this rising sign, and she may be a wonderful role model and a great support, or difficult, demanding, and selfish. Worse still, she could damage the subject psychologically. Either way, this subject cares about his mother and wouldn't want to see her suffer, but the attachment to the mother can be so great that it can

become a problem for the person's partner, especially if the mother sets out to bully the partner.

This subject may be the oldest child in the family or the one who has the most responsible attitude, and he will carry much of the emotional and financial burden for his siblings and other relatives during

Cancer: Put It All Together

••••••◆◆◆◆◆••••••

Cancer is a feminine, cardinal, water sign, which makes it confusing even to itself, but this person can't be pushed far.

much of his life. He may be a late developer but does well later in life as he has common sense and a certain amount of shrewdness. This person is interested in such things as heritage, history, and possibly also in visiting stately homes or collecting antiques.

The Cancer rising person can be moody and ill tempered, downhearted, or worried, but the greatest problem is a lack of confidence, especially when dealing with difficult situations and difficult people. The subject's outer manner is pleasant and nonthreatening, but he can be unpleasant when he feels himself to be under attack—sometimes when there is no actual attack. Under severe pressure, he will go home and shut out the world, retreating crabwise into this shell until he feels able to cope again. Most of the time, however, he is friendly, hospitable, and helpful.

With Leo on the second house cusp, this subject can earn good money at times, but he can also spend large amounts of it on entertaining guests, on travel, and on luxuries.

Leo Rising

This subject may be the oldest child in the family—or the only girl in a family of boys or vice versa. His parents wanted him and they tried to do their best for him. It is likely that the subject was talented in music, acting, or art, and possibly also quite a good-looking child; whether this translates

into success later in life depends on other factors. One thing is sure: he will always love his own children and do his best for them.

This subject may have had a difficult father, possibly one who was very pleased with himself. The parents might have found the child talkative, slow, irritating, expensive, or just in the way, so he was sometimes pushed aside or resented. This subject's main fault is vanity and self-centeredness. He is a good friend who can be sociable and amusing, kind and pleasant. He works hard and wants to succeed.

With Virgo on the second house, the person is shrewd and cautious where money and possessions are concerned.

Leo: Put It All Together

This is a masculine, fixed, fire sign, and thus quite hard to change, but this makes him loyal and apt to stay in situations longer than he might need to.

Virgo Rising

It is hard for this person to win the approval of his parents. These children often have loud voices and a demanding manner. They can be sick much of the time, often with nervous ailments, and they can be fussy about food, clothes, their room, and much else.

This is a very intelligent sign, but in some cases it is hard for these people to get anywhere in life, due to a fear of failure, or perhaps even a fear of success! The Virgo rising person comes across to others as organized and rather serious, and as long as he doesn't get bees in his bonnet, he eventually sorts himself out and has a good life. In time the loud voice and difficult manner vanishes, and the Virgo rising person becomes a good and very reliable friend, with a great sense of humor. He may succeed in personal relationships, but usually not until later in life when he meets someone who appreciates his oddball ways and intense loyalty. He is an excellent parent, but possibly a bit pushy and ambitious for his children. Where work is concerned, he does well in accountancy, property development, business, or, oddly enough, in the media or on the stage. There are many Virgo rising people in publishing.

These people are careful with money but with Libra on the second house cusp, they can be surprisingly ready to spend money on the things that give them pleasure, such as music, art, clothes, beauty treatments, or home décor.

Virgo: Put It All Together

The feminine, mutable nature of this sign makes them appear flexible, but earth signs are stubborn, so they aren't as easygoing as they might appear.

Libra Rising

Childhood may have been fairly easy although it is likely that the subject's parents were somewhat neglectful, possibly giving him things in place of the attention he really needed, or they may have wanted him to achieve more than he was capable of. This individual may use his good looks and charm to extricate himself from sticky situations, and he may use it to get by in life as he can be somewhat lazy. He dislikes coarseness and unpleasantness, but he appreciates art, music, and nice surroundings.

His pleasantness and refinement make him excellent company, and he would do well in a job where these qualities matter, such as running an art gallery or an executive catering business. He is a good cook and homemaker and a great host. His sense of justice and his ability to bring people together may take him into the law or some form of agency work or arbitration. He needs a strong partner who can help him cope, but he can make a mess of relationships by being unnecessarily confrontational or unreliable. He might be a flirt, or just attractive to others.

With Scorpio on the second house cusp, this subject is surprisingly careful over financial matters, and he can even help others to organize or maximize their own funds.

Libra: Put It All Together

This is a confusing sign, as it is masculine, yet ruled by the most feminine of planets, which is Venus. It is a cardinal sign, which means Libra rising people do their own thing and can't be pushed around, but it is also an air sign, so these people are great to talk to and exchange ideas with, but they may not get too much off the ground.

Scorpio Rising

This subject was loved and wanted, but he was born into or surrounded by some difficult situation, which made him feel out of step with others. This situation breeds a cautious attitude and a variety of deep feelings that this person keeps hidden from the world outside. He is intuitive and uses this when assessing others, and may also use it in his job, so he could be drawn to something like the law or forensic work. He could also be drawn to the armed forces. He may work in an advisory capacity where things like money, mortgages, and insurance are concerned.

He has a friendly manner and wants to be liked, but his real friends are few and far between. He may be loyal in relationships and a good family member—or utterly unable to stay with any one person for long. He is a caring parent but not a particularly consistent one, and he can be demanding and fussy, which makes life difficult for those around him.

With Sagittarius on the second house, this individual can be surprisingly foolish where money and possessions are concerned.

Scorpio: Put It All Together

This is a strong sign, ruled by Mars, but it is also a feminine sign, so it can put up with a lot. Being a water sign, the subject is intuitive, and this may lead him into mediumship, astrology, and so on.

Sagittarius Rising

This subject's childhood was reasonable, but his desire for freedom and adventure led him to leave home early and he may have experimented with different lifestyles before settling down. If he was brought up in a family or school that emphasized a particular religion or set of beliefs, he will question them and find his own belief system later.

This person has a kind heart and good intentions, but is too restless to be relied on. He projects an image of intelligence and friendliness and shows an interest in everyone and everything around him, but those who seek to lean on him will soon find that he has—like Elvis— "left the room."

Many astrologers and people who are interested in spiritual matters have this rising sign, and their knowledge can be encyclopedic. Similarly, many people in the world of religion or philosophy also have this sign on the ascendant. Teaching and learning come easily to this subject, and he is almost bound to teach, instruct, or coach others during the course of his life. He is great fun and can be very entertaining, and he really can light up a room with his charisma and sense of humor. Some of these people go into the world of entertainment.

Sagittarus: Put It All Together

Being a masculine, mutable, fire sign, this restless character must keep on moving, learning, and doing things as long as he is able.

Oddly enough, this individual may have excellent building skills, so he could be someone who works in this field and travels from place to place for his work. Indeed, he is bound to travel as part of his work or simply to get out and about and be part of the wider world.

With the sign of Capricorn on the second house, this subject can be surprisingly canny about money, and even if he suffers financial setbacks in life, he will find a way to recover and become financially secure once again.

Capricorn Rising

Someone with this sign rising grew up in difficult circumstances. He is loved and wanted, but there may be poverty or loss, a sick father, or too many other children in the family. He learned early to save money and to take life seriously. It is possible that he was ailing, possibly with an autoimmune disorder, such as asthma or eczema, which meant he missed out on some school activities. Even if that isn't the case, he wasn't an athletic child. However, his diligence and intelligence means he will do well later in life.

His outer manner is serious and he may seem older than his years, but he has a good sense of humor that saves him from being a prig or a bore. He is ambitious and he sees no need to sit around moaning when there is work to be done. He is efficient, capable, and useful to an employer. This person could go into business of any kind, but he is likely to work in or manage a large organization or project in the course of time.

He is a loyal and loving partner and a good parent who takes his duty to his family seriously. He looks after his parents and other older members of his family when he starts to get somewhere in life, when he becomes financially stable.

His second house is in the unpredictable sign of Aquarius, so he may make gains and losses of goods, money, and possessions at times during his life.

Capricorn: Put It All Together

••••◆◆◆◆◆◆•••••

This is a cardinal sign, so this person might be quiet and unassuming on the surface, but he is hard to push around. It is also a feminine earth sign, which gives endurance.

Aquarius Rising

This person's parents loved him and did their best for him, although there may have been a lack of money, sickness in the family, or some other problem. His father may have been sick or may have left the family. The subject learned to be independent early on, partly because it was necessary for him to be so, and partly due to a combination of an independent nature and parents who encouraged him to be himself. He did well enough at school, not so much in academic subjects, but in sports and technical subjects.

He may go into teaching as a profession, or into something technical that requires an inventive mind and a love of originality. He might pursue local or national politics.

This person is intelligent and also tougher than he looks, and while charming and popular, he is also hardworking and very ambitious. However, he is also quite idealistic and humanitarian, and he wants the best for others as well as for himself.

He is a good family man who looks after all the other members of his family as well as he can. He may be unpredictable at times, but his heart is in the right place. He projects an image of coolness and doesn't like to show emotion or weakness. He travels a lot, by choice and also due to his career, and he likes meeting people from a variety of backgrounds.

> ### Aquarius: Put It All Together
>
> ••••••◆◆◆◆◆◆••••••
>
> This is a masculine, fixed sign, so this subject finishes what he starts and upholds the status quo, but it is also an air sign, so he enjoys the world of ideas and meeting a variety of people.

With his second house in Pisces, his finances may fluctuate at times, but he is cautious where money is concerned and always has something to fall back on.

Pisces Rising

For technical reasons of astronomy, Pisces is an unusual rising sign, although it is somewhat more common in the southern hemisphere than it is in the UK or the US.

This person's childhood was probably difficult, either due to problematic family circumstances or due to illness. Indeed, many people with this sign rising spend time in a hospital when young, which removes them from their family and makes them lonely. Alternatively, they may be lonely at school or may spend time at home on their own. Whatever

the circumstances, they learn to develop their own inner resource, which in turn develops their imagination. This draws these folk into the worlds of spiritualism, mediumship, and other New Age interests, but it also helps them develop their creativity, so they become writers, poets, musicians, actors, artists, and so on later in life, although usually as a hobby rather than as a career.

Some people with this rising sign are very sporty, and this can be a compensation for them if they don't do well in academic school subjects. Oddly enough, they often have an aptitude for figures, and they always have an aptitude for business. They are often attached to the creative or mystical world, but in a business capacity, perhaps as publishers or running spiritual businesses. They are restless, so they might work in the travel trade or in some job that involves driving and vehicles.

Pisces has the reputation of being a weak and gentle sign, but these people can have a prickly and hostile manner born out of a feeling that they need to defend themselves against others, normally when nothing of the kind is the case. They are helpful when they want to be, but they can suddenly turn and become unpleasant when in a bad mood.

With the second house in Aries, these people can always find a way to make money or gather possessions, often in the form of property or premises, and they don't spend too freely either, so they can end up being quite wealthy.

Pisces: Put It All Together

On the face of it this should be a losing sign, as it is feminine, mutable, and of the water element, but it is strong, possibly because these people develop so much on an inner or spiritual level rather than leaning on others.

❋ ❋ ❋

5

THE ASTROLOGICAL HOUSES

The rising sign is the starting point for the twelve houses. There are various different systems in use but the simplest is the equal house system, which means that all the houses are exactly the same size. One important word to know to understand the houses is *cusps*. A *cusp* is the point where two signs or houses meet.

Angular, Succedent, Cadent

The first, fourth, seventh, and tenth houses are angular, which makes them stronger than the other two kinds of houses. The second, fifth, eighth, and eleventh houses are succedent, so they tend to follow on the decisions taken by the planets in the angular houses. The third, sixth, ninth, and twelfth houses are cadent houses, which bring things to a close.

The First House

Being so close to the rising sign, this house refers to the programming the person received in childhood and it affects the person's outer manner. It is associated with the person's appearance, manner and image, and some health issues. This can show talents and perhaps career or lifestyle.

The Second House

This house is concerned with values, the person's image, and personal possessions and personal finances. His basic security needs, as well as self-esteem and the way he is valued by others, are shown here, as are some abstract priorities such as security, love, and freedom. This also shows whether such concepts as décor, beauty, the arts, music, cooking, or gardening figure in the subject's life. This house can rule land, or money in the bank.

The Third House

This house is associated with siblings, neighbors, close friendships, and also the locality the person lives in. It rules communications, information, and figure work, along with the way the subject thinks and speaks. It rules his basic education and level of dexterity. Local travel, short journeys, and mode of transport are ruled by this house.

The Fourth House

This house rules mother figures, the childhood home, and domestic circumstances, including the subject's home, land, and property or business premises. It is mainly concerned with the home and family matters, but interests in the past and such things as history, antiques, and family heritage are shown here.

The Fifth House

This house covers artistry, creativity, and especially music, and the creation of a family (especially children), a business enterprise, a work of art, or a book. This is associated with pleasures, holidays, hobbies, and games that are fun and amusing, including fun-filled love affairs and time off from the realities of daily life.

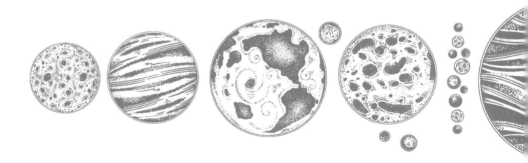

The Sixth House

This house rules employers and employees, work and duty of all kinds. Health, prevention of illness, and anything to do with fitness are indicated here. This could show an interest in health matters and complementary therapies and so on. It can also show a tendency to overwork or to be lazy.

The Seventh House

Traditionally this is the house of marriage, but this can rule any close partnership that is aboveboard, including business partnerships. The seventh house also rules agreements, contracts, and justice. Open relationships can include enemies! A sense of justice or injustice can be seen here, as well as anything to do with the law and legal matters.

The Eighth House

This is concerned with shared finances and resources, either personal or business. It rules dealings with financial institutions, legacies, taxes, corporate matters, and even the police or judiciary. Birth, death, sex, and karma are associated with this house as are secrets, resentment, pain, transformation, and hidden or occult matters. This house shows those things that make the person resentful or that seem to oppose him in life, such as coming up against authority or other abstract concepts.

The Ninth House

This rules travel over distances (rather than local travel), foreigners, foreign goods, and different cultures. Issues of freedom, independence, and exploration can be shown here. Anything that expands the person's intellectual horizons, such as higher education, religion, or philosophy. Justice and the law can be important here. Traditionally, this house also rules gambling and luck. It is associated with animals, especially large ones.

The Tenth House

This house can indicate the career, but it really represents any goal or ambition. Parents, especially father figures, are ruled here, as are authority figures. Status, public acclaim, political advancement, and anything else that happens outside the home or in the public gaze are ruled by this house. This can connect to big business or government in some way.

The Eleventh House

This house rules detached relationships, such as friendships, clubs, societies, and group activities, so it is a social house. It also links with local government and things that benefit the people in the individual's locality. The acquisition of knowledge and original or unusual ideas is here, as are intellectual pastimes and astrology. This is the house of originality. It also rules hopes and wishes for the individual and for those around him.

The Twelfth House

This house can show where the person makes sacrifices or cares for those who need help. It rules places of seclusion such as prisons and hospitals or even working quietly at home. It also connects with mysticism, hidden matters, hidden enemies, secrets, and feelings of insecurity. Planets in this house can lend artistry, musical talent, or psychic ability to the person, but they can also denote a person's undoing or some form of self-destructive behavior.

SIGN AND HOUSE CONNECTIONS

◆

The signs run from Aries through Pisces, the houses run from one to twelve, and each sign has a similar character to each house, so once you understand the character of each sign, you will also have a grip on the way that each house works. The following shows the connections between each of the signs and houses and the things that each is concerned with:

Sign	House	Connections
Aries	First	The self and the body
Taurus	Second	What is valued, personal finances, possessions
Gemini	Third	Communication, local matters
Cancer	Fourth	Home, family, mother, the past
Leo	Fifth	Children, fun, creativity
Virgo	Sixth	Work and health
Libra	Seventh	Love relationships, work partnerships, opponents
Scorpio	Eighth	Shared resources, financial partnerships, sex, resentment
Sagittarius	Ninth	Expansion, education, philosophy, travel
Capricorn	Tenth	Status, goals, ambitions, career matters
Aquarius	Eleventh	Friendships, hopes, wishes
Pisces	Twelfth	Hidden matters, vulnerability, self-undoing

✻ ✻ ✻

6

THE MOON SIGNS

The moon orbits the earth every 27.3 days, but it moves from one degree of the zodiac to the next every 29.5 days. The moon sign is less obvious than the sun sign, as it rules reactions rather than actions, and it concerns the hidden and inner side of the personality. Most importantly, it relates to the emotions and to behavior that is determined by the way we are.

A subject's inner nature won't always be obvious to outsiders, and even those who are close to the person may not be totally aware of the person's real feelings, but the subject will definitely be aware of them, even if he can't always put them into words. In some ways, it reveals the person's true inner motives and inner personality, however well these may be hidden.

The moon sometimes has something to say about the relationship to the parents, especially the mother. It can refer to the home and domestic circumstances, but it can also show whether the person is in tune with the needs of the public.

The Moon and the Genders

If we refer back to the chapter on the zodiac, you'll have noticed that the gender of the signs doesn't affect the sun signs that much, but when we consider the gender of the *moon sign*, the gender has a definite impact. People who have the moon in masculine signs are less sensitive and less impressionable than those with the moon in feminine signs.

Sign	Aries	Taurus	Gemini
Gender	♂	♀	♂
Sign	Cancer	Leo	Virgo
Gender	♀	♂	♀
Sign	Libra	Scorpio	Sagittarius
Gender	♂	♀	♂
Sign	Capricorn	Aquarius	Pisces
Gender	♀	♂	♀

KEY	Masculine ♂
	Feminine ♀

The Moon and the Elements

Similarly, when it comes to the elements, the moon sign really comes into its own, as the person's reactions to a situation can be very different from their outward manner or behavior, so it is worth noting what is on the inside when dealing with others. This becomes most noticeable when life goes against these subjects, and when they find themselves up against it—as we will see in a moment.

Fire signs	Aries, Leo, Sagittarius
Earth signs	Taurus, Virgo, Capricorn
Air signs	Gemini, Libra, Aquarius
Water signs	Cancer, Scorpio, Pisces

Fire Sign Moon

The positive side of this moon sign is that the person doesn't suffer as much on an emotional level as some of the other types, so he has a happier life. However, the person with the moon in Aries or the moon in Sagittarius is unlikely to get much sympathy or help from his parents, so he has to make his own way in life.

Negatively, when annoyed or upset or when a relationship or job doesn't work out the way the person wishes, the fire moons can lash out and hurt others without considering the consequences. These people are optimistic enough to be able to walk out of a situation in the belief that they will soon find another job, home, partner, or lifestyle—and they probably will. The moon sign that is most likely to hang on in a difficult situation is someone with the moon in Leo, because that is a fixed sign. This person's parents are active and successful.

Earth Sign Moon

The positive side of this moon is that these people tend to commit to the relationships that are important to them and they don't walk away from

anything that easily. The person who is most able to move away from difficulties and adapt to new circumstances is the one with the moon in Virgo, because that is a mutable sign.

Negatively, when under pressure, these people hang on to everything they've got with every fiber of their being. When relationships break down, they fight hard in the divorce court for material possessions. They fear destitution, so money in the bank means a great deal to them. The parents are hardworking.

Air Sign Moon

On the positive side, these subjects can climb the ladder of success and get ahead in life in a way that others can only envy. They feel that they are cleverer than others—and they often are, so they win when others flounder and give up. These people are tough, independent, and able to weather all manner of storms.

They love their families deeply but have only a few really important friends. Their parents are intelligent but often self-educated.

Water Sign Moon

On a positive note, many of these folk work as counselors, as psychics, or in the social and civil services, helping out in disaster areas wherever and whenever specialist help is needed. These people understand others and can offer friendship or give solace in a way that others can't, but they may not be able to do so day after day, so it isn't a good idea to lean on them too much.

Negatively, these people suffer deeply and feel their own inner pain, hurt, and resentment on a grand scale. They feel that life should be much easier and better than it actually is, and this can make their behavior extreme.

The Moon and the Qualities

The three qualities are cardinal, fixed, and mutable. They play out in the moon sign in ways that aren't always obvious, but they are there nevertheless.

Cardinal signs:	Aries, Cancer, Libra, Capricorn
Fixed signs:	Taurus, Leo, Scorpio, Aquarius
Mutable signs	Gemini, Virgo, Sagittarius, Pisces

Cardinal Sign Moon

When the moon is in a cardinal sign, the person won't be pushed around, so can make a success of a job or of some other aspect of life where others struggle. These people consider themselves important and can be real winners. They look after their families and loved ones by providing money and goods for them. However, when challenged, they argue, fight back, and don't mind hurting others, so they can be difficult to live with. On the other hand, they aren't ground down by difficult people, because they don't allow others to dictate to them.

Fixed Sign Moon

This person has a powerful sense of responsibility and can put up with a lot. He will stay in situations longer than most, sometimes for practical rather than emotional reasons, such as enjoying a wealthy lifestyle. This subject can become too fond of his own ideas and opinions, so he might get out of step with everyone else. On a positive note, in a world where there is little commitment to others, either in working life or in personal relationships, this person can make and keep a commitment.

Mutable Sign Moon

These people are intelligent and capable, but they aren't always strong enough or determined enough to be great winners in the game of life. They may sound strong and they can reach the top, but when push comes to shove, they may back down when it would be better to stand firm. Some are happy to agree with the last person they happened to be talking to. If things get too difficult, this person can get very ground down, but he might simply up and leave, soon finding a more congenial situation.

The Moon through the Signs

The rest of this chapter is devoted to the individual moon signs.

Moon in Aries

This person thinks and talks quickly and can cope with large-scale plans, although he may need help when it comes to getting things done. His enthusiasm and energy needs an outlet in meaningful work, where he feels that what he is doing matters. Women of this sign are good homemakers, but they also need an interesting job outside the home. The relationship with the parents may have been difficult and there may have been furious arguments, especially with the father. Partnerships can also be stormy as this person won't give way or compromise.

Moon in Taurus

This person can deal with practical problems, but emotional problems are a different matter. He has a pleasant, friendly, sociable manner and he is reliable and kind, but he can also be difficult. He may have a tricky relationship with his parents. This subject has a sensual nature that makes him enjoy art, nature, and travel. He can be stubborn, but he is consistent. He needs money in the bank and a roof over his head and will work hard to provide these things for himself and his family.

Moon in Gemini

The mind is active, logical, and businesslike. The individual reads a lot and stores up knowledge, and also loves to travel. This subject is fairly cool in some ways, but if he gets upset it goes inward and makes him ill. If he loves someone, his feelings are deep and he is totally loyal. He will do all he can to ensure that his children receive as good an education as he can afford. Being a hard worker, this person can always earn money when the need arises.

Moon in Cancer

This person is emotional, sensitive, and moody, but may
seek to hide this from outsiders. He may be imaginative
and creative, and he appreciates music and the arts.
Being naturally intuitive, he may be drawn to psychic or
mystical matters, but he can be equally at home in the
worlds of teaching or business. He is good to his family
and loves domestic and family life, but can be clannish. He will be moody at
times and can get ill when he is unhappy. This subject has a good memory and
may be fond of historical topics.

Moon in Leo

This person puts on a display of confidence even if he
doesn't feel confident, because he hates to look stupid or
inadequate. He likes being in the center of things. He can
be very responsible or totally irresponsible, absolutely
honest or a wonderful crook. He can sacrifice a lot for his
family and children. He may put his relatives or children
on a pedestal, or he may be very fond of himself. Being
excellent organizers and businesspeople, these folk take advantage of trends
and opportunities as they arise, so they can be very successful. They don't like
their own company much, so they have lots of friends.

Moon in Virgo

This subject is keenly intellectual, discriminating, and
capable of dealing with details. He is also ambitious
and determined, but he can find emotions getting in
the way at inopportune moments. At work he can be
comfortable in a secondary position, as long as his
efforts are appreciated. He is likely to be a good cook
and homemaker, and he may be fond of small children
and pets. Some prefer to stay single because their career takes precedence over
matters of love, but others are simply rather detached. However, there are
plenty of subjects who enjoy family life. Many dislike displays of affection, but
they are kindhearted and loving in their own quiet way.

Moon in Libra

Being charming, optimistic, outgoing, and sociable, this subject is a skilled and tactful diplomat who is usually popular at work and in social settings. This is a tough moon sign, so this person is not as soft as he might appear, due to being ambitious, hardworking, and determined, especially when he has a goal in sight. This individual isn't keen on his own company, so friends, relatives, and lovers are all welcome additions to his home and his life, but he needs to come and go without being questioned. Those who seek to monopolize or drain him will soon be rejected. He is faithful when in the right relationship, but this doesn't prevent him from flirting.

Moon in Scorpio

The emotions are close to the surface and there is a wellspring of resentment here. The family background will be difficult and this person may seek to escape as soon as he can, but he may find it hard to break away completely. It is possible for him to hold down a mundane job, but this will be balanced by hobbies or leisure interests that have real meaning. If at all possible, this individual will find fulfilling work that is important to others. He prefers to be in a meaningful relationship and is unlikely to let a partner down, but he won't forgive someone who is disloyal to him.

Moon in Sagittarius

This subject may work as an astrologer or in the psychic and spiritual field, while others work in religious fields, because this person's moon urges him to find something meaningful in his life. His parents may have followed a religion or set of beliefs, but when the subject grows up, he looks around and finds his own belief system. This person needs freedom but he can sustain a relationship over a period of time; he is likely to take on a lame duck or someone who is difficult. There is a fair chance that pets or even large animals will become a feature in this person's life.

Moon in Capricorn

Childhood experiences will have shown this person that
life can be very hard, as there may have been bereavement,
poverty, or hardship in the home. It takes this subject a
long time to get anywhere in life, but he is ambitious, so his
application and determination mean that he quietly climbs
the ladder of success. He looks after his family well, and as

he tends to have a long life, he eventually makes up for the shortages and setbacks
of his earlier years. He isn't particularly outgoing, so he is probably shy, especially
in emotional matters. This subject has a talent for detail and has a good memory.

Moon in Aquarius

This subject's early life was not easy, not
through bad parents or a lack of love, but due to
difficult circumstances, so this leads him to work
hard in order to make a success of himself. This

individual cannot be dictated to because he needs to plough his own furrow.
He may take up an unexpected career or make a success of a difficult one due
to his courage and determination, and he can face up to disasters better than
most. His independent and unusual nature can make him hard for others to
understand, and his self-sufficiency might make it difficult for him to maintain
close partnerships. He will have plenty of friends, though.

Moon in Pisces

This is a very sensitive moon sign. The individual's
values are a mixture of the spiritual and the
materialistic, so he may choose an unusual lifestyle that
allows him to explore both sides of his nature. Many
with this moon sign work in the psychic sciences, and
many serve in religious or spiritual organizations. This

subject can be influenced by the feelings of others and
become angry or unhappy when there is no reason for him to be so, simply
because he is picking up on the emotions of those around him.

Childhood experiences leave a mark, making this person vulnerable,
sensitive, and easily hurt, which leads him to be helpful to others when they
need someone to turn to.

✳ ✳ ✳

7

THE PLANETS

Mercury

Mercury is the smallest and innermost planet, and its orbital period around the sun of eighty-eight days is the shortest of all the planets in the solar system. It is named after the Roman deity Mercury, who was the messenger to the gods.

Due to this planet's close proximity to the sun, Mercury will be in the same sign as the sun or one sign behind or ahead of the sun. So, for example, someone born with the sun in Sagittarius could have Mercury in Scorpio, in Sagittarius, or in Capricorn.

There are times when the earth appears to be overtaking Mercury, and this happens on average three times a year for a period of two to three weeks; when this happens, we say that Mercury is retrograde. From our point of view as astrologers, we know that this is a time when communications go wrong, vehicles and local travel can cause problems, our health may let us down, and things may get lost.

In astrology, Mercury is concerned with basic education, literacy, numeracy, and communications of all kinds—and also with the area in which people live and work, local travel, and everything attached to daily life, such as running errands. Mercury rules writing and figure work; buying, selling, and marketing; and such things as buses, taxis, and the family car. It also is concerned with relationships with brothers, sisters, cousins, and neighbors. This is also the planet of illness, health, and healing, and if a person is into magic, this is his planet. It can relate to movement and thus to some forms of sport, such as running and hiking. Mercury also rules tricksters and thieves.

When Mercury is in a sign or a house, this is how it plays out:

Sign or House in Mercury	
Aries/First House	Quick thinking, active, competitive, sporty, humorous, possibly sarcastic.
Taurus/Second House	Thorough, capable, clever with finances.
Gemini/Third House	Quick thinking, great communicator, can be somewhat neurotic.

Sign or House in Mercury (Continued)	
Cancer/Fourth House	May work from home. May work with family members.
Leo/Fifth House	Good at games and business. Well organized.
Virgo/Sixth House	Logical, analytical, clever, may be fussy.
Libra/Seventh House	Attracted to the arts. Good agent. Needs a companion to talk to.
Scorpio/Eighth House	Deep, quick mind. Good investigator. Interested in mental or physical health.
Sagittarius/Ninth House	Broadminded. Good with the hands. Enjoys travel.
Capricorn/Tenth House	Slow but thorough thinker. Banking, business, and money appeal.
Aquarius/Eleventh House	Original mind. Unusual relatives. Can speak without thinking enough.
Pisces/Twelfth House	Great ideas, but are they practical?

Venus

Venus is the second planet away from the sun and has an orbit of 224 days. Because it is closer to the sun than the earth is, it is often found in the same sign as the sun or in the previous or following sign. It can fall into a sign that is two away from the sun sign, if one of the two planets is at the very end of a sign and the other at the very beginning of one.

Venus relates to the things one possesses and values, which means that it is often taken to refer to money, as this is the means by which people obtain possessions. However, it need not be attached to finances but to other things that are of value or importance, such as, the home, personal freedom, or things that are beautiful in the subject's eyes. Venus shows the way a person gives love and what he wants from a lover. This is also the planet of luxury, relaxation, and having a good time. It can also show the way someone dresses and presents himself to the world.

Sign or House in Venus	
Aries/First House	The person's own needs count and he may be possessive.
Taurus/Second House	Sensuality, a love of beauty, creative talent.
Gemini/Third House	Books, ideas, contact with others. Friendships may be easier than relationships.
Cancer/Fourth House	Home, family, background are important.
Leo/Fifth House	Children, lovers, fun, music. A creative outlet is vital.
Virgo/Sixth House	Books, productive work. Loyal but not possessive.
Libra/Seventh House	Love, luxury, pleasure, beauty. Also, a need for justice.
Scorpio/Eighth House	Very possessive, passionate, deep. Money is vital for this individual's happiness.
Sagittarius/Ninth House	Personal freedom is vital. Truth and ideas are valued.
Capricorn/Tenth House	Ambitious, materialistic. Achievement is valued.
Aquarius/Eleventh House	Friendship with influential people. Education is valued.
Pisces/Twelfth House	Art, music, creativity. Mystical matters and love are valued.

Mars

Mars is the next planet in line after the earth. A Mars year
is twice as long as ours, and Mars has two moons. This
planet shows how a subject goes after what he wants, and it
expresses the assertive, masculine side of the person's nature.
It can show the way someone acts when they have a crush on someone and
what they do to obtain love and sex. The Romans called Mars the god of war,
so it shows what a person can fight for. Mars shows how the individual uses his
energy and for what purpose.

Sign or House in Mars	
Aries/First House	Decisive, active, sexy. May work in a field that helps the community.
Taurus/Second House	Thorough, creative. Able to finish what is started.
Gemini/Third House	Talkative, intelligent. Will work with computers or as a communicator.
Cancer/Fourth House	Good at do-it-yourself. Will put energy into family life and a family business. A wimp!
Leo/Fifth House	Salesmanship, hard worker, charismatic, childish.
Virgo/Sixth House	Hard worker, good mind, talkative, interested in health and healing.
Libra/Seventh House	A great lover, materialistic, luxury loving, good arbitrator.
Scorpio/Eighth House	Very sexy, intense, possessive, secretive.
Sagittarius/Ninth House	Religion and philosophy important. Good at sports. Enjoys travel.
Capricorn/Tenth House	Ambitious, hard worker, clever scientist or mathematician.

Sign or House in Mars (Continued)	
Aquarius/Eleventh House	Good student or teacher. Friendly, humanitarian. Works for the common good.
Pisces/Twelfth House	Creative, romantic. Good swimmer. Dreamer. May be religious.

Jupiter

Jupiter is the first of the really distant planets, and it spins far more quickly than the earth. It consists of gas, dust, and stormy clouds. Jupiter has around fifteen moons but only four of these are sizable.

The sign that Jupiter was in at birth will throw considerable light on a person's beliefs and value system. This also determines how adventurous the person is and the way he attempts to expand his horizons. Jupiter in some signs inclines the person to be a gambler or risk-taker, and in others it breathes life into what otherwise might be a dull personality. Jupiter is a wonderful indicator of where and how a person is likely to find luck.

Sign or House in Jupiter	
Aries/First House	Strong beliefs, values truth, loves travel. Can make money by his own efforts.
Taurus/Second House	Legal or spiritual work may provide a living. The subject should take care not to overspend.
Gemini/Third House	Talking or writing will bring luck and an income.
Cancer/Fourth House	A wealthy background perhaps, or luck through property.
Leo/Fifth House	Creative work and children bring luck. Lucky winner but big spender.

Sign or House in Jupiter (Continued)	
Virgo/Sixth House	Work brings luck, but original ideas can also prove lucky.
Libra/Seventh House	Luck through marriage or partnerships.
Scorpio/Eighth House	Legacies, marriage, or divorce bring luck.
Sagittarius/Ninth House	Travel and exploration are lucky. Spiritual matters fascinate this person.
Capricorn/Tenth House	Career advancement likely as is success in science or politics.
Aquarius/Eleventh House	Luck comes in unusual ways or through friends.
Pisces/Twelfth House	The subject's values are spiritual rather than material.

Saturn

Saturn, the very distant and very beautiful ringed planet, has many satellites, some of which are large enough to be called moons. Dour old Saturn is the planet that all student astrologers love to hate. It represents restrictions and limitations, and its position shows where one's greatest hardships and life lessons lie. However, it is often by overcoming these hardships that we learn to create a structure to our lives and to win through. Saturn represents hard work and attention to detail. It also signifies old age and happiness in later life.

Sign or House in Saturn	
Aries/First House	A difficult early life but hard work pays off later. Quiet and modest.
Taurus/Second House	It takes time to accumulate money and possessions. Plenty of common sense.
Gemini/Third House	Early education is poor or unpleasant. Success later through writing and teaching.
Cancer/Fourth House	Stressful early life, difficult parents. Good home life later.
Leo/Fifth House	Children may be a burden. May work too hard.
Virgo/Sixth House	Much work and sacrifice on behalf of others. Possible poor health.
Libra/Seventh House	Marriage to a much older or younger partner. Successful work relationships.
Scorpio/Eighth House	Success in business and with finances after a tough start.
Sagittarius/Ninth House	Must guard against being too opinionated. Travel for business and fame far from home.
Capricorn/Tenth House	A tough start but fame and success as long as he avoids dishonesty. Strong parents.
Aquarius/Eleventh House	Friends may influence the subject's career or make use of him.
Pisces/Twelfth House	One of the parents was difficult. This subject should avoid lame ducks.

Uranus

This planet was discovered in 1848. It spins in a different direction
to all the other planets, and its poles are at the side rather than in
the north/south position. It is a gas giant.

Uranus is the "breakout" planet. It breaks the rules and causes
upheavals in people's lives. In a birth chart, Uranus rules creativity, originality,
and sometimes psychic gifts. It is associated with higher education, science,
new inventions, and new ideas—and also with friendship and other detached
relationships, political ideas, and personal freedom. It also rules hopes and wishes.

Sign or House in Uranus	
Aries/First House	Rebellious, independent, or eccentric. Friendships are important.
Taurus/Second House	Fluctuations in goods, money, and possessions. Unusual talents.
Gemini/Third House	An unusual or disrupted education. A talent for communicating.
Cancer/Fourth House	Unusual family or home circumstances. An unusual home setup.
Leo/Fifth House	Gifted children, unusual talents. Luck with gambling or sports.
Virgo/Sixth House	May have two jobs or unusual interests. Talented.
Libra/Seventh House	Several marriages, ups and downs in life due to partnerships.
Scorpio/Eighth House	Sudden gains and losses due to events concerning others.
Sagittarius/Ninth House	May marry a foreigner or travel to strange places. Many friends.

Sign or House in Uranus (Continued)	
Capricorn/Tenth House	Unusual career or dual careers. Humanitarian and idealistic.
Aquarius/Eleventh House	Many friends, wide-ranging interests. Could be an astrologer.
Pisces/Twelfth House	Intuitive, psychic, artistic, musical. Unusual lifestyle and odd friends.

Neptune

Neptune is a very distant gas giant. In astrology, it is associated with the sea and travel, but also with dreams, imagination, creativity, and escape from humdrum life. It relates to psychic matters, intuition, mysticism, religion and spiritual ideas, also to art, music, and all that makes life pleasant. However, there is a dark side to Neptune: it makes it hard for people to see the truth of things, and can cause muddles, misunderstandings, illusion, and self-delusion, but also sudden revelations. This planet rules escapist behavior through drink or drugs or by running away, but it also relates to kindness and a good heart.

Sign or House in Neptune	
Aries/First House	Creative, artistic. May never get their act together.
Taurus/Second House	Strange ups and downs regarding wealth and possessions.
Gemini/Third House	Clever with words, may be a medium. Work and education are unstable.
Cancer/Fourth House	Home life is confusing and the family may be difficult.

Sign or House in Neptune (Continued)	
Leo/Fifth House	Talented, has sensitive children who are also talented.
Virgo/Sixth House	Attracted to work in health or healing. Kind-hearted.
Libra/Seventh House	Very happy or miserable in relationships. Must avoid rescuing lame ducks.
Scorpio/Eighth House	Money comes and goes depending on the actions of others.
Sagittarius/Ninth House	Travel over water or a home by the sea brings luck and peace.
Capricorn/Tenth House	May work in an artistic, musical, or spiritual field. May advise and counsel others.
Aquarius/Eleventh House	Oddball friends bring inspiration and fun. An unusual lifestyle.
Pisces/Twelfth House	Very artistic and dreamy, but the subject needs to keep track of reality. Mystical and possibly religious.

Pluto

Pluto is technically a dwarf planet, which at the moment is inside the orbit of Neptune. Pluto has one very large moon called Charon (pronounced Sharon), which makes it a binary planet.

Pluto rules transformation, even to the point of destroying things so that it can rebuild in a better way later. Because of its association with union and dependent partnerships, it is associated with shared resources, big money, and such things as taxes, mortgages, and legacies. Union can also imply sexual relationships and the big family issues of birth and death, gains and losses. It can also relate to recycling, where something is no longer used for its original purpose. This planet rules deep thinking and deep feelings.

Sign or House in Pluto

Aries/First House	Politician or leader with power for good or ill.
Taurus/Second House	Can become extremely wealthy—or lose the lot.
Gemini/Third House	Wonderful communicator who can make money from writing or teaching.
Cancer/Fourth House	Powerful family, for good or ill. The past exerts a strong hold.
Leo/Fifth House	Children or enterprises transform the person's life.
Virgo/Sixth House	Can achieve much on behalf of others. May be a workaholic.
Libra/Seventh House	Marriage can bring great gains or losses.
Scorpio/Eighth House	Legacies, mortgages, taxes, corporate matters, and marriage bring luck or losses.
Sagittarius/Ninth House	A wish to improve the world. Foreign ventures or emigration bring money.
Capricorn/Tenth House	Public success and power, but setbacks are possible.
Aquarius/Eleventh House	New and revolutionary ideas bring success. Powerful friends are helpful.
Pisces/Twelfth House	Very psychic, good healer. Hard life but keen to help others.

Chiron

Chiron is a dwarf planet that astrologers have been using since the late 1970s. It rules health and changes in partnerships and relationships, but its most important feature is that it shows where the deepest psychological wound lies.

Sign or House in Chiron	
Aries/First House	May have problems with headaches. May not be physically attractive. May lack confidence, but eventual success helps to build self-esteem.
Taurus/Second House	Money, possessions, or appearance may be lacking. May have weak throat or neck. Development of common sense prevents over-extravagance.
Gemini/Third House	May struggle at school, have problems getting around, or dislike neighbors. Bronchitis possible. Adult education and training put things right.
Cancer/Fourth House	May dislike home surroundings or family. May have weak lungs or breast problems. Earns good money in later life.
Leo/Fifth House	May have problems with younger members of family. May be unlucky gambler. Weak spine. Music and entertaining others brings happiness later.
Virgo/Sixth House	Work may be hard or health weak. Problems with bowels. Finds love eventually and health improves when older.
Libra/Seventh House	Partnerships can be difficult. Problems with kidneys, pancreas, or bladder.

Sign or House in Chiron (Continued)

Scorpio/Eighth House	Work or personal partnerships can be difficult. Resentment possible. Problems in reproductive area of body. Helping others brings friendship and affection.
Sagittarius/Ninth House	May struggle with belief system or philosophy. Foreigners troublesome. Health problems in hips and thighs. Finds own belief system.
Capricorn/Tenth House	May struggle with career or with older men in the family. Weak knees, shins, and calves. May find success in a job where music is important.
Aquarius/Eleventh House	May struggle with education, lack of good friends. Weak ankles. Politics or humanitarian work is successful.
Pisces/Twelfth House	May be isolated and lonely. Health problems with the feet. Succeeds in a creative field.

✳ ✳ ✳

8

THE
ASPECTS

The aspects between planets can be beneficial and helpful or stressful and difficult, although the difficult ones can also be character-building. Some aspects aren't too bad, but they can sometimes be hard to live with.

Major Aspects

The major aspects are always worth using, because they have a profound effect on a person's life.

The Conjunction
0 TO 10 DEGREES APART

The conjunction occurs when two planets are close to each other, in this case within 10 degrees of each other. The conjunction should be a helpful factor on a chart, but it can be depressing or a cause of resentment, depending on which planets are involved.

The Sextile
60 DEGREES APART WITH AN ORB OF 6 DEGREES

This is a helpful aspect, and it works in a logical or intellectual, rather than an emotional or romantic way.

The Square
90 DEGREES APART WITH AN ORB OF 6 DEGREES

Squares are stressful but they can be character-building.

The Trine
120 DEGREES APART WITH AN ORB OF 6 DEGREES

The trines are beneficial and their influence is creative or even loving.

The Opposition
OPPOSITE EACH OTHER AT 180 DEGREES APART
WITH AN ORB OF 8 DEGREES

Oppositions involve interaction with others, and these interactions can be helpful or difficult, depending on the personalities involved.

Minor Aspects

These aren't as powerful in their effect as the major aspects, but they can be surprisingly helpful or awkward at times, so they are worth checking out on your own chart or the charts of your loved ones.

The Semi-Square
TWO SIGNS THAT ARE 45 DEGREES APART,
WITH AN ORB OF 3 OR 4 DEGREES

This slightly stressful aspect can bring opposition to one's plans, or delays and setbacks.

The Semi-Sextile
TWO SIGNS SIDE BY SIDE AT 30 DEGREES APART WITH
AN ORB OF 3 OR 4 DEGREES

Despite the fact that the two signs are of a different gender, element, and quality from each other, this aspect is mildly beneficial. Adjacent signs have a slight similarity to each other, and people often have the sun in one sign and planets in adjacent signs, which also helps.

The Inconjunct
TWO PLANETS 150 DEGREES APART

The two signs have nothing in common, being of a different gender, element, and quality, which makes this an awkward aspect. This aspect can make working relationships, health, finances, joint financial matters, or important relationships difficult.

The Yod, or Double-Inconjunct

This strange word applies to a situation where there are two inconjuncts to one planet. It can be a really challenging aspect that affects health, relationships, and finances at times.

The Quintile
TWO PLANETS 72 DEGREES APART

This shows intelligence and talent linked to the planets and signs in question.

✻ ✻ ✻

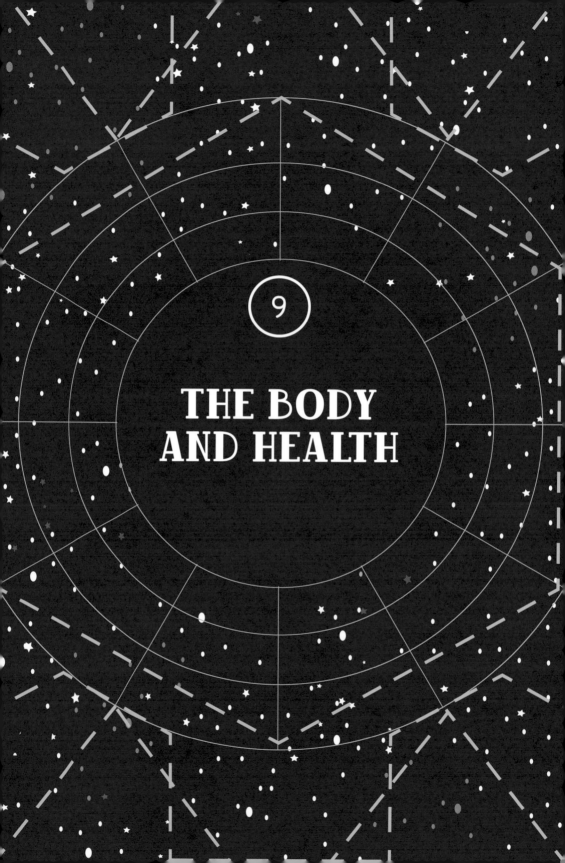

THE BODY
AND HEALTH

Signs by Tradition

Tradition tells us that the signs of the zodiac rule parts of the body, starting with Aries at the head and Pisces at the feet. Each planet is associated with one or two signs, and thus also rules some part of the body. Taken as a whole, health and astrology is a big subject, but here is a brief guide to the system.

Aries and Mars

Aries and Mars rule the head, eyes, face, lips, upper teeth, and even the hair, which can have a reddish hue. Mars is associated with accidents, fevers, and sudden onset of illness. Aries is a self-indulgent sign, so these people may overeat or overdo alcohol. The best outlet for them is competitive sports. There is a tendency to heart trouble and leukemia later in life.

Taurus and Venus

Taurus and Venus rule the cheeks, neck, throat, lower teeth, vocal chords, and nose. This also links with the ability to get around. Venus is also associated with

An Illustration of the Astrological Body from the Early Fifteenth Century

Libra. Venus is activated when colds and coughs strike, and also when whiplash injuries occur. Taurus can overindulge with sweet foods, so weight gain can be a problem. To relieve tension, Taurus should take up gardening and do-it-yourself projects or dance and walk to keep weight down. As long as this person doesn't smoke, the chances of a long life are good.

Gemini and Mercury

Gemini and Mercury rule the shoulders, arms, wrists, hands, bronchial system, nerves, brain, pupils, and the tip of the tongue. Mercury is also associated with Virgo. Mercury turns retrograde two or three times a year, and this is when health problems can suddenly occur. Visiting nice places and enjoying pleasant walks is good for the Gemini nerves, as are light sports such as badminton, bowling, and pool. The tendency to bronchitis could lead to pneumonia in some cases.

Cancer and the Moon

Cancer and the moon are linked to the breasts, lungs, chest, and digestive system. Swimming, horse riding, and walking are all good exercise for this sign, as is something amusing like line-dancing. Any sign of cancer, especially breast cancer, must be treated quickly.

Leo and the Sun

Leo and the sun rule the spine, heart, and solar plexus. This sign and planet can be associated with pregnancy. Exercise such as swimming, skating, skiing, dancing, or playing in the park with one's children can help this sign, as can a decent diet and a good vacation once in a while. Heart attacks are possible with this sign due to a buildup of cholesterol. These people shouldn't smoke.

Virgo and Mercury

Virgo and Mercury rule the abdomen, intestines, bowels, nerves, and skin. Mercury is also associated with Gemini. Eating proper meals rather than snacking is advised. Aromatherapy, massage, or  anything that soothes the nerves is good, as is gentle exercise, such as yoga or gardening, and having fun with friends. This person should take those checks for bowel cancer if something seems to be wrong. Diabetes is also possible for this sign

Libra and Venus

Libra and Venus rule the lower back, haunches, bladder, kidneys, and pancreas. Venus is also associated with Taurus. Librans like to dance, and light sports such as golf, fishing, pool, and badminton will  also help to keep this sign healthy. Librans like an alcoholic drink, and as long as it isn't too much or too often, that's fine. The throat may be at risk of cancer if this person smokes. Diabetes is fairly common for this sign.

Scorpio and Pluto

Scorpio and Pluto rule the reproductive organs, sexual organs, and duodenum. Resentment and anger can play a part in the health of this sign or planet. Scorpio should take up competitive exercise, such as fencing  or some kind of football. This sign also needs to avoid eating too much spicy or oily food. The digestion is delicate, so it could be at risk of cancer, and the arteries are susceptible to a buildup of cholesterol.

Sagittarius and Jupiter

Sagittarius and Jupiter rule the hips, thighs, sciatic nerve, and liver. Problems with this sign or planet can restrict the person's ability to get around. This is an active sign that likes playing games and sports, and

most Sagittarians eat sensibly as well, so health shouldn't be much of an issue. Mental health is another issue, though, because many Sagittarians take on too much or get burdened by family members who take advantage of them and wear them out. The liver is delicate, so this person shouldn't be a heavy drinker.

Capricorn and Saturn

Capricorn and Saturn rule the knees, bones, joints, teeth, hearing, breathing, body hair, and skin. Capricorns need to take calcium and vitamin D on a regular basis, and they need to walk, dance, play light sports, run around the park with their children, and try not to worry so much. This person should live a long life, but worry can lead to heart problems over time.

Aquarius and Uranus

Uranus and Aquarius rule the calves, ankles, blood pressure, breathing, and circulation. This sign is associated with sudden change, so illness or accidents may occur unexpectedly. This isn't a particularly unhealthy sign, but these people need to keep active in some sport that doesn't hurt the ankles. Yoga, tai-chi, karate, or judo might appeal. This person is apt to get varicose veins and leg ulcers, so shouldn't smoke and should keep sugary foods to a minimum to avoid diabetes.

Pisces and Neptune

Pisces and Neptune rule the feet, toes, instep, mental state, and lymph glands. Pisceans have a tendency to gain weight, so they should eat a good balanced diet and walk, swim, or dance as much as possible.

Many Pisceans are excellent dancers and rhythmical music makes them happy, but some would enjoy tai-chi or yoga. Some Pisceans are heavy drinkers but very few are smokers. However, the main problem is weight gain in middle and later life.

❋ ❋ ❋

10

PREDICTIVE TECHNIQUES

Methods

There are many methods of astrological prediction but the useful ones boil down to four, and these are the ones we will take a look at here. They are:

1. Transits: a method that every astrologer uses.
2. Progressions: a popular method, if only to check on what the progressed moon is up to.
3. Returns: also known as solar and lunar returns. These are interesting, but not as useful as the previous two methods.
4. Electional astrology, which has a different purpose than the other three.

As a reminder, here are the glyphs for the signs:

Aries ♈	Taurus ♉	Gemini ♊	Cancer ♋
Leo ♌	Virgo ♍	Libra ♎	Scorpio ♏
Sagittarius ♐	Capricorn ♑	Aquarius ♒	Pisces ♓

Below are the glyphs for the planets. There are a few other things on the chart, such as the nodes of the moon, ascendant, midheaven, and so on, but this at least is the planetary list, which should help you while you're getting the hang of astrology.

The sun ☉	The moon ☽	Mercury ☿	Venus ♀
Mars ♂	Jupiter ♃	Saturn ♄	Uranus ♅
Neptune ♆	Pluto ♇	Chiron ⚷	

Transits

Transits are the movements of planets and the constellations that are in the sky at any particular moment, so if you look at the sky at night and know which planets and constellations are which, this is what you would also see listed in an astrological ephemeris (book of tables) on the astrology chart for that day as shown on your app or astrology software.

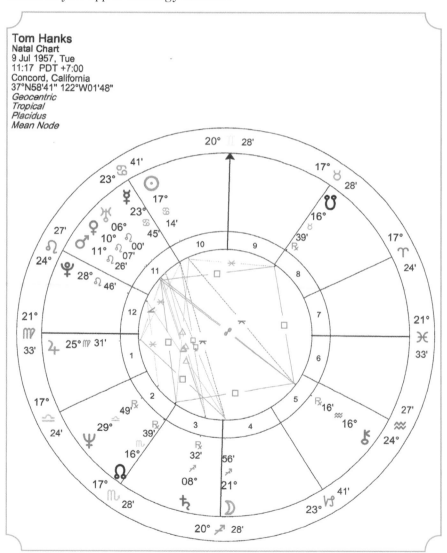

Tom Hanks's Birth Chart

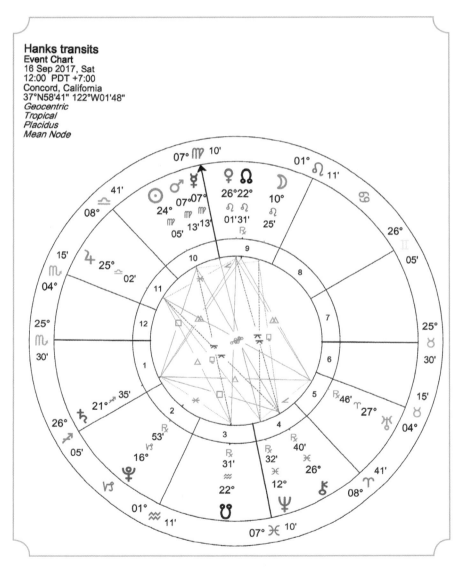

In theory, you could make up two chart wheels—one for the birth chart and another for the transit chart—but that makes it hard to work out what's happening. The best way is to set up a biwheel, which places the birth chart in the middle and the transit chart outside. Here is the situation for Tom Hanks, which I have shown first as a two-wheel and then as a biwheel situation.

Hanks transits
Event Chart
16 Sep 2017, Sat
12:00 PDT +7:00
Concord, California
37°N58'41" 122°W01'48"
Geocentric
Tropical
Placidus
Mean Node

Tom Hanks's Transit Chart

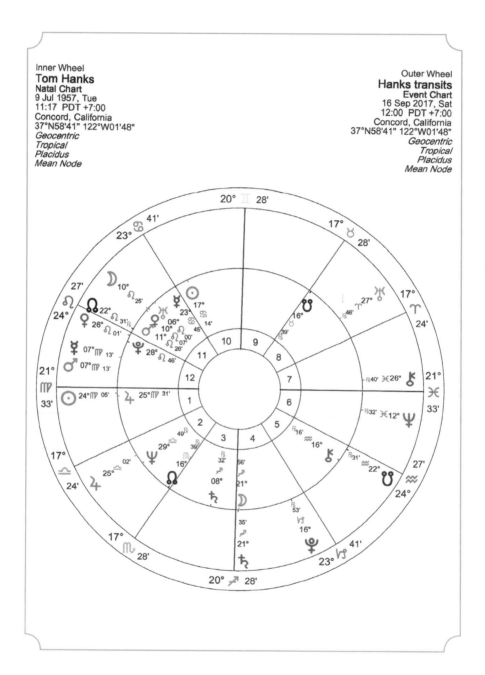

Tom Hanks's Birth Chart with Biwheel Transit Chart

Using this method, you can look back to any date within the person's lifetime, check out the current situation, or check out any date in the future.

Tom Hanks's Transits

Original Birth Data	
Date of birth:	July 9, 1956
Time of birth:	11:17 local time
Place of birth:	Concord, California, USA

I have set the transit chart for the day that I happen to be writing this, which is September 16, 2017, and I have set it for Tom's place of birth at Concord and with the time set for midday.

STARTING POINT

The transit chart is *outside* the natal one, so that's the one we are looking at. I start at the ascendant and work my way round the chart in a counterclockwise direction. Tom's ascendant is in the hardworking sign of Virgo, and you will see that the first house is just below the ascendant.

I won't give Tom a complete interpretation as it would take too long and make this chapter boring, but I will make a start to set your feet on the right road. So now let's see what planet or feature comes up first after the ascendant.

The Astrology Clock

Astrology programs use the 24-hour clock, so you don't have to worry about whether something is a.m. or p.m.

Looking at the outer wheel, the first planet you see is the sun, which is at 24° of Virgo. The sun takes a month to travel through each sign by transit, so at the moment it is close to the end of Virgo and will soon be on its way to Libra. When the sun is in the first house, it signals a time of optimism and might indicate that young people, such as grandchildren, are involved in Tom's life right now. The ascendant would have passed by the sun earlier that day, marking an optimistic time of new beginnings. The solar effect suggests there is something coming along that is well worth doing, so it seems that by chance I've picked an interesting time for our unwitting volunteer.

Now take a look at the degree that the sun is at and see if it lines up with anything on the birth chart. The transiting sun is at 24° of Virgo, so working round the chart, it makes the following aspects:

The transiting sun is just coming into an exact conjunction with Jupiter, which is considered a "lucky" planet. Jupiter is a planet that enlarges and expands horizons and makes anything the person is doing more successful than ever. Transiting Jupiter is 25 degrees of Libra, and therefore coming into a conjunction with Neptune, and as Neptune rules film and entertainment, this bodes well for Tom at this time.

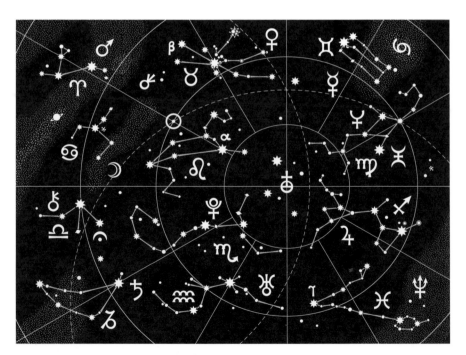

Zodiac Constellations

Transiting Saturn is almost in an exact conjunction with the moon, being only twenty-one minutes of a degree away from it, so something purposeful is happening within Tom's household or his family. This might actually be a mixture of an event that signals success and achievement, but Saturn being what it is, this can also be a slightly depressing time for Tom. Perhaps he is looking back to times when his family situation was different from the current circumstances.

More importantly, transiting Pluto is opposite to Tom's natal sun, signaling a time of transformation. Tom's natal sun is in his tenth house of attainment and achievement, but Pluto is currently transiting his fourth house of home and family. Saturn crossing the moon combined with this Pluto opposition hint that changes are happening within Tom's home life, and they may not be easy to live through. I could speculate that he has the builders in and it is getting on his nerves.

The fact that the north and south nodes of the moon have recently connected with natal Pluto reinforces the sense of domestic upheaval. So the feeling so far from this reading is that Tom's career is forging ahead but that his home circumstances are temporarily askew.

If you now look around the rest of the chart, you will see the following:

- Transiting Neptune at 12 degrees Pisces, making an inconjunct to natal Mars.
- Transiting Chiron at 26 degrees Pisces, making an opposition to natal Jupiter.
- Transiting Uranus at 27 degrees Aries, making a trine to natal Pluto but an inconjunct to natal Jupiter.
- Transiting Mars at 7 degrees Virgo, making a square to natal Saturn.

In short, this seems to be a time of great activity for Tom, with the usual mix of nice things and difficulties that are so much part of life for every one of us.

I have ignored the moon, Mercury, Venus and the sun, as they move too quickly to make much impression, but if you were doing this for yourself, you would want to take every planet into consideration, along with the transiting ascendant, midheaven, and anything else that captured your attention.

Progressions

Some astrologers call this *day-for-a-year progressions* and some call it *secondary directions*. I call it *progressions*. The idea is that you progress the chart from its position on the day of birth forward by as many days as the years that have passed since the person was born. So someone who is twenty-one years old would have a chart that is progressed by twenty-one days, while in the case of Tom Hanks, who is sixty-one, the chart has to be progressed by sixty-one days. This is easy to do with any halfway decent astrology program.

When working with transits, the important planets are the slow-moving outer planets, because the inner ones move too quickly to make much impression on the person, but where progressions are concerned it is the other way around. For instance, Saturn, Uranus, Neptune, and Pluto won't move far enough during many years to make any difference to the chart. In the case of a young person, even Jupiter won't have had time to go far. In addition, when a planet is retrograde by progression, its progress will be so slow as to almost be brought to a halt.

Work the system in exactly the same way as you did for the transits, starting at the ascendant and focusing on those planets and features that have moved enough to make an impact. Mercury is at 11° of Libra, which shows that it has recently passed by a trine aspect with both natal and progressed Chiron in Aquarius. Both Chiron and Mercury relate to health issues and Libra talks about partnerships, so it is possible that someone who loves Tom has urged him to take extra care of himself, maybe as a result of a health scare.

The most useful planet in progressed astrology is the moon, as it shows what is going on at the time of the reading. It moves forward a degree every month, so it is easy to check out the sign, house, and aspects it will form over a specific period of time.

Solar Returns

A solar return is a chart that is set for the moment when the sun returns to the exact position that it was in when someone was born. This is the reason we say "Happy Returns" when someone has a birthday!

This is actually a *transit* chart that is set for the time and day of the solar return. It isn't an important method of prediction, but it gives what I call a *feeling* or an *atmosphere* of the year in question. If your software can cope with solar returns, check out a few of these from your own past and see how accurate they were.

Electional Astrology

If you have something important coming up and there is some flexibility about the day and time on which you can do it, you can set up dozens of charts and find the best one for the purpose. In practice, it doesn't work very well, as there is rarely enough leeway to find the best moment. Also, while there may be several really good aspects, there are always a few dodgy ones as well. In addition, fate has a habit of messing up one's plans, however carefully we make them. There is an old Jewish proverb that goes "Man makes plans and God laughs," and that is often the case where this kind of astrology is concerned.

Lunar Returns

There are also lunar returns, which take the chart back to the point where the moon was at the time of birth. These occur every lunar month. While they only give an atmosphere of a particular month, they can be interesting to play around with. My experience is that they kick in a little before the actual date of the return, and start to fade before the next lunar return.

11

LOVE AND COMPATIBILITY

One of the things the public loves to ask is what sign they are compatible with. The answer is that it depends on each individual chart, but some aspects between the two sun signs can give a clue to the potential for success—or otherwise. However, here are a number of ideas to ponder, starting with the most basic kind of data.

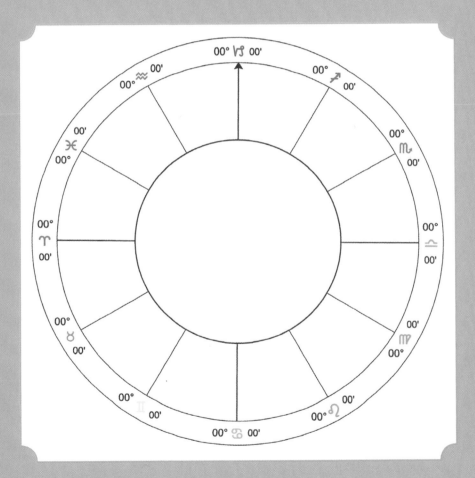

The Signs of the Zodiac

Simple Sun Sign Connections

Same Sign—Conjunction

It is obvious that we understand people of our own sign, but this connection is more common as a family connection or for friendship than it is for love.

Two Signs Away on Either Side of the Sun Sign—Sextile

This is an easy connection as both signs are the same gender and they share compatible elements, such as fire and air, or earth and water. There is often a similarity in the way these people think and behave.

Three Signs Away on Either Side of the Sun Sign—Square

This is a tense connection although the signs share the same quality. There may be a sexual attraction.

Four Signs Away on Either Side of the Sun Sign—Trine

Every sun sign book or magazine article picks this one as being the ideal relationship. In truth, the two signs share a gender and element, so they have much in common but the quality will be different. The trines link the fire signs of

The Opposite Sign

••••◆◆◆◆◆◆••••

This is a common connection for lovers, partners, friends, and colleagues—and often a very successful one. The signs share the same gender and quality, and although their elements are different, they are compatible with each other; for instance, fire and air, or earth and water. Depending on factors in both charts, however, the connection can be completely negative. The oppositions are Aries/Libra, Taurus/Scorpio, Gemini/Sagittarius, Cancer/Capricorn, Leo/Aquarius, and Virgo/Pisces.

Aries/Leo/Sagittarius, the earth signs of Taurus/Virgo/Capricorn, the air signs of Gemini/Libra/Aquarius, and the water signs of Cancer/Scorpio/Pisces.

Five Signs Away on Either Side of the Sun Sign—Inconjunct

This is unlikely to work.

The Moon Connection

Some people link on a lunar level, so it's worth checking out the sign that the moon is in. There may be a connection on an emotional level between people with the same moon sign or signs with the same quality. The link between genders and elements doesn't seem to be as important as the qualities here.

Venus and Mars

There can be connections between Venus and Mars. This doesn't seem to be very important in love connections, though it can be useful where work is concerned.

The Midheaven

The midheaven can be an important connection and often a very successful one as far as committed relationships are concerned. Any app or software will show the sign on the midheaven. This is always somewhere at the top of the chart; the symbol for the midheaven is MC or Mc.

The Vertex

This is an extremely sensitive point on the chart, expressed as VX or Vx. It shows where a subject will encounter deeply emotional situations that can turn life upside down for good or for ill. The nature of the relationship and the events it sets off will be influenced by the sign in question. In a birth chart, this can make a particular sign very important, whereby people notice a connection to those with the sun, moon, or ascendant in that sign, even if not actually conjunct the vertex. When you get into predictive astrology, you can check transits and progressions that make important aspects to the vertex.

❋ ❋ ❋

12

EASY
MISCELLANY

Cusps

A *cusp* is the point between two signs or two houses. A planet on the cusp may be at the very end of a sign or house or at the very beginning of a sign or house.

Abbreviations	
Asc: Ascendant	Dsc: Descendant
Mc: Medium Coeli or Midheaven	Ic: Imum Coeli or Nadir, Lower Midheaven
ACG: Astrocartography	LSA: Local Space Astrology

Why Twins Are Not Always the Same

In some cases twins are very alike, but in others they are very different, and this is regardless of whether they are identical or fraternal. If astrology is such a surefire way of judging a person's character and lifestyle, what accounts for this anomaly?

A simple answer—and one that is often very true—is that there are many factors and features on a birth chart, and one twin can express one part of the chart while the other twin expresses another.

However, here is a more technical answer. The Asc changes by one degree every four minutes, which means that a twelve-minute difference in time of birth will give a three-degree difference to the Asc. This could push the Asc into another sign, or it could bring it into an aspect with a planet. It will make the house cusps slightly different, and more importantly, the exact position of the Mc will be different. All of this can cause a slight difference in the character and behavior of the two twins.

Twins are usually brought up in the same household, go to the same school, and live the same kind of lives while growing up. They often marry and have children at similar times and in similar circumstances. Many also remain close to each other throughout life.

Much the same data works for other multiple births—that is, each child is similar to the others, but not exactly the same.

A SET OF REAL TWINS

The Kray twins were notorious British gangsters. Their charts are given as 8 p.m. and 8:10 p.m. which sounds as though the times have been rounded up, but nevertheless, Reginald Kray was definitely the older of the two by

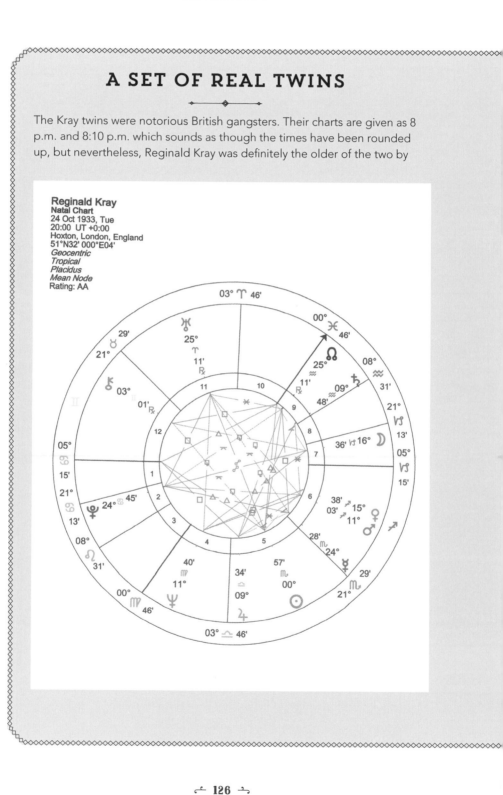

Reginald Kray
Natal Chart
24 Oct 1933, Tue
20:00 UT +0:00
Hoxton, London, England
51°N32' 000°E04'
Geocentric
Tropical
Placidus
Mean Node
Rating: AA

ten minutes. Note the slight difference in the numbers for the Asc, Dsc, Mc, Ic, and the houses. Note also that Ronald Kray's Mercury and Saturn are in different houses from those of his older brother, and there is an additional inconjunct on Ronald's chart that runs from the Asc to Saturn.

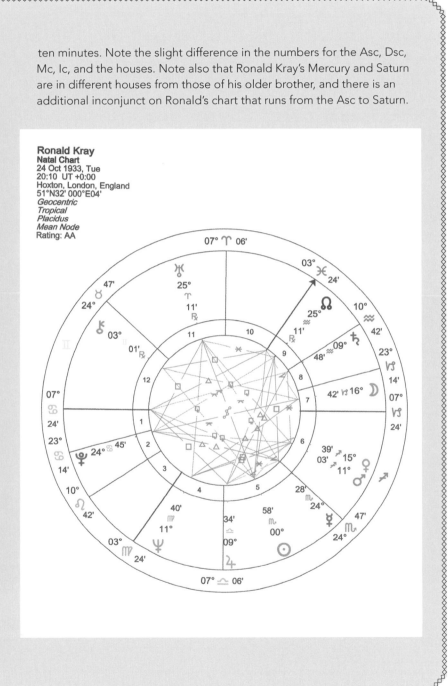

Ronald Kray
Natal Chart
24 Oct 1933, Tue
20:10 UT +0:00
Hoxton, London, England
51°N32' 000°E04'
Geocentric
Tropical
Placidus
Mean Node
Rating: AA

Astrological Twins

Astrological twins are two people born on the same day, near to each other in distance and close in time. The theory is that these people will have a similar horoscope and lifestyle, and I have found this to be true, with the events of each pair's childhood and early life being very similar.

Decans

Each sign of the zodiac contains thirty degrees, and in the system that some call *decans* and others call *decanates*, the signs are split into three sections, each containing ten degrees. When you look at the various members of your own family, you will see links between relatives by sign and decan. It is possible to work the system by date rather than by degree but only roughly, as the cusps might be a bit ragged.

The System by Degree
First decan: $0°$ to $9°$
Second decan: $10°$ to $19°$
Third decan: $20°$ to $29°$

The System by Date
First decan: The start of a sign to the end of the month.
Second decan: The 1st to the 10th of the month.
Third decan: The 11th to the end of the sign.

The first decan sub-rules the sign by itself, the second sub-rules it by the next sign along in the same element, and the third decan sub-rules it by the next one after that in the same element, going round and round the system until each sign has been dealt with. The full list of decans is shown below.

Decans	
Aries—Fire Element	Aries/Aries Aries/Leo Aries/Sagittarius
Taurus—Earth Element	Taurus/Taurus Taurus/Virgo Taurus/Capricorn
Gemini—Air Element	Gemini/Gemini Gemini/Libra Gemini/Aquarius
Cancer—Water Element	Cancer/Cancer Cancer/Scorpio Cancer/Pisces
Leo—Fire Element	Leo/Leo Leo/Sagittarius Leo/Aries
Virgo—Earth Element	Virgo/Virgo Virgo/Capricorn Virgo/Taurus
Libra—Air Element	Libra/Libra Libra/Aquarius Libra/Gemini
Scorpio—Water Element	Scorpio/Scorpio Scorpio/Pisces Scorpio/Cancer
Sagittarius—Fire Element	Sagittarius/Sagittarius Sagittarius/Aries Sagittarius/Leo
Capricorn—Earth Element	Capricorn/Capricorn Capricorn/Taurus Capricorn/Virgo

Decans (Continued)	
Aquarius—Air Element	Aquarius/Aquarius Aquarius/Gemini Aquarius/Libra
Pisces—Water Element	Pisces/Pisces Pisces/Cancer Pisces/Scorpio

Dwaads

Dwaads are similar to decans but each sun sign is split into divisions of two-and-a-half degrees, each of which is called a *dwaad*, which is a word taken from Hindu or Vedic astrology. The first dwaad is a repeat of the sign itself and the rest follow in turn, ending with the sign that precedes the sun sign. Here by example is the situation for Gemini:

First dwaad:	Gemini/Gemini
Second dwaad:	Gemini/Cancer
Third dwaad:	Gemini/Leo
Fourth dwaad:	Gemini/Virgo
Fifth dwaad:	Gemini/Libra
Sixth dwaad:	Gemini/Scorpio
Seventh dwaad:	Gemini/Sagittarius
Eighth dwaad:	Gemini/Capricorn
Ninth dwaad:	Gemini/Aquarius
Tenth dwaad:	Gemini/Pisces

Eleventh dwaad:	Gemini/Aries
Twelfth dwaad:	Gemini/Taurus

If you have a head for mathematics, you will soon spot that the first four dwaads are a breakdown of the first decan, while the second group is a breakdown of the second decan, and the third is a breakdown of the third decan. So what use are these systems? Well, the decan system really does work, but whether the dwaads are much use might be a moot point.

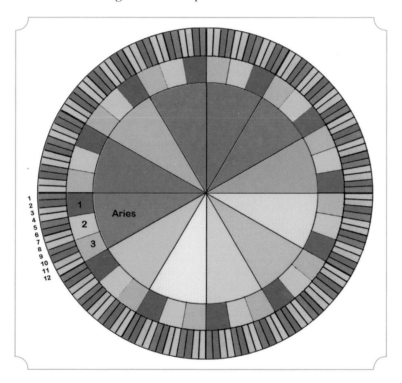

The innermost circle shows the signs.
The middle circle shows the three decans for each sign.
The outer circle shows the twelve dwaads per sign.

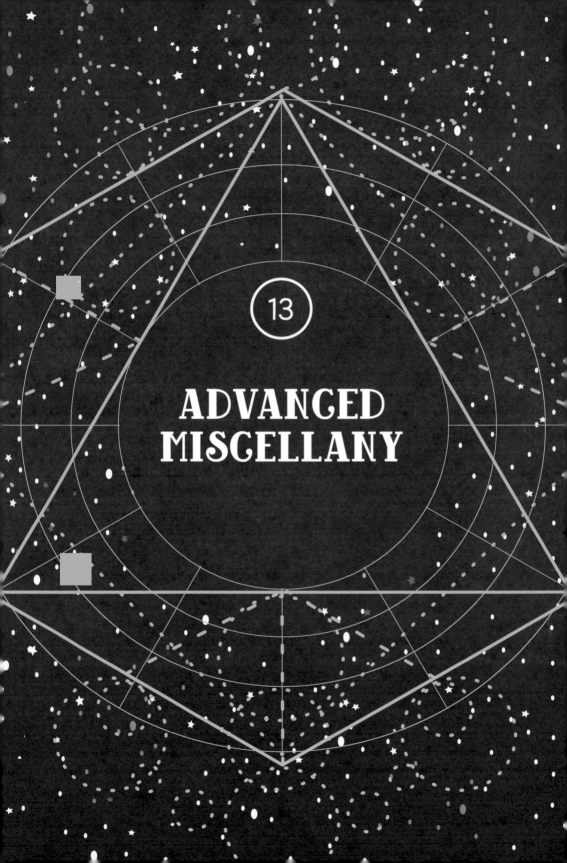

13

ADVANCED
MISCELLANY

Why Is the East in the West?

When you look at a chart, you will see the Asc on the left-hand side, and this is called the eastern horizon, but the ascendant appears to be in the west. Well, the answer to this question is remarkably simple.

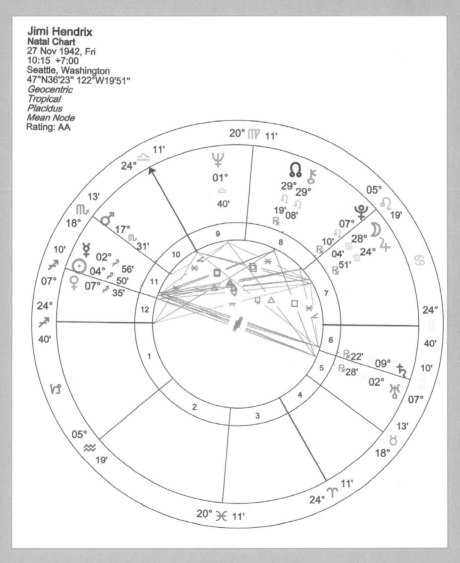

Jimi Hendrix's Birth Chart

Way back in history (with the exception of some Aztecs perhaps), the only people with enough education to study astronomy and astrology lived in the northern hemisphere, and they worked on their charts as though they were facing south toward the sun and the ecliptic. So, if you are living in the northern hemisphere now, pick up your birth chart and hold the paper upright while facing toward the south, and now you will see that east is east and west is west. In addition, the Mc is at the top of the sky and the Ic is on the other side of the earth.

Long and Short Ascension

We know that the earth turns on its axis once in every twenty-four hours, and it would make life nice and easy for astrologers if each sign took two hours to rise, but the earth is only upright when you look at it in an atlas, because the reality is that its axis is 23.43 degrees from the perpendicular. This means that the ecliptic is at an angle to the equator, making some signs appear to zoom upward in a very short time and others to take much longer. This effect becomes more exaggerated the farther one travels from the equator. If one visits either the North or South Pole during summer, the sun never sets, whereas in the depths of winter it never rises, so at these times the ascendant is nowhere to be seen!

If we now add the time of the year factor, this makes some signs pass by quickly and others more slowly, again due to the relationship between the earth, the solar system, and the constellations. In England, the sign of Cancer can take almost three hours to go by at certain times of the year, while the sign of Pisces takes only forty-five minutes at most, and as little as fifteen minutes at other times of the year. This makes Cancer a common rising sign and Pisces an extremely uncommon one in the UK. The situation is the same in any other country once you reach latitudes of over forty-five degrees north.

This is the pattern in England, much of the USA, and the northern hemisphere in general:

Aries: Short	Taurus: Middling	Gemini: Long	Leo: Long
Cancer: Longest	Virgo: Long	Libra: Longish	Scorpio: Middling
Sagittarius: Shortish	Capricorn: Shorter	Aquarius: Short	Pisces: Shortest

The southern hemisphere reverses, because Capricorn becomes the sign of longest ascension and Virgo the shortest. Here is the pattern once you move away from the equator:

Libra: Short	Scorpio: Middling	Sagittarius: Long	Capricorn: Longest
Aquarius: Long	Pisces: Long	Aries: Longish	Taurus: Middling
Gemini: Shorter	Cancer: Short	Leo: Short	Virgo: Shortest

Retrograde Planets

The ancients believed that the sun orbited the earth, but we know it is the center of the solar system and we are one of the planets that orbit it. The effect is that sometimes we appear to be moving faster than one of the other planets, which has the effect of making the planet look as if it is moving *backward* through the sky. This is called *retrograde motion*. You will see it on some systems with a letter R and a line through the tail or the retrograde planet will be colored red in transit and progressed biwheel charts.

The sun and moon are never retrograde, but the planets all turn retrograde from time to time. The outer planets from Jupiter to Pluto are retrograde when the sun is more or less opposite the sign that the planet is in. The reason for this is that the earth is always in the opposite sign to the sun, and as we travel much more quickly than the outer planets, we pass them by in the same way that an express train passes by a much slower local one, so it looks as though the planet is traveling backward. The reasoning is a bit different with the inner planets, and the sun doesn't need to be in an opposing sign for them to be retrograde.

If you look at Jimi Hendrix's chart, in addition to the nodes, you will see Uranus, Saturn, Jupiter, and Pluto all retrograde. Added to a number of square and opposing aspects on Jimi's chart, it is obvious that this lovely, talented man's life was extremely troubled right from the start.

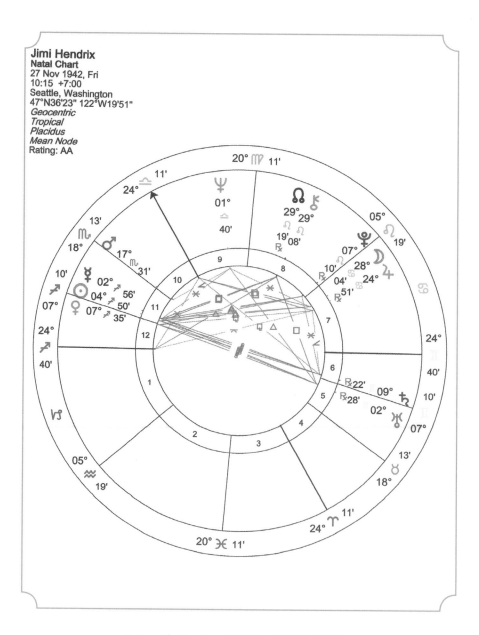

Jimi Hendrix
Natal Chart
27 Nov 1942, Fri
10:15 +7:00
Seattle, Washington
47°N36'23" 122°W19'51"
Geocentric
Tropical
Placidus
Mean Node
Rating: AA

Retrograde Planets on Jimi Hendrix's Birth Chart

Nodes of the Moon

The moon crosses the ecliptic on an upward trajectory, and two weeks later it crosses it on a downward journey; then after another two weeks, it crosses upward again and so on. These crossing points are called *nodes*. The symbols for the nodes look like hooks and eyes, with the north node upright and the other reversed. Jimi's chart shows only the north node, but it's easy to see where the south node would be, as it is exactly opposite the north node.

The theory of the nodes comes from Hindu astrology, where the north node is called *Rahu*, which means the dragon's head, and the south node is called *Ketu*, which means the dragon's tail. The theory is that the south node relates to our past lives and, therefore, shows areas of life that we find easy to cope with (because we've been there before), whereas the north node shows lessons we need to learn in our present incarnation. This seems to work reasonably well, but I have noticed that if someone is born with either node in conjunction with a planet on their birth chart, the person will become famous for something and, depending on the planet in question, they may also become rich.

Some Western astrologers say that doing something when the transiting north node is in conjunction with a natal planet makes life easy, and that things started at that time go well, and vice versa for the south node. Strangely, there are Asian and Oriental systems that say the *absolute opposite*, and I have come to the conclusion that they are right.

I have also noticed that transits to the nodes kick off matters related to the family and also to property and premises, both working premises and the home, in particular, the kitchen.

Nodes of Planets

All planets other than the sun cross the ecliptic every once in a while, although it might take a few centuries in some cases for this to come about, but most astrologers don't worry about theses nodes.

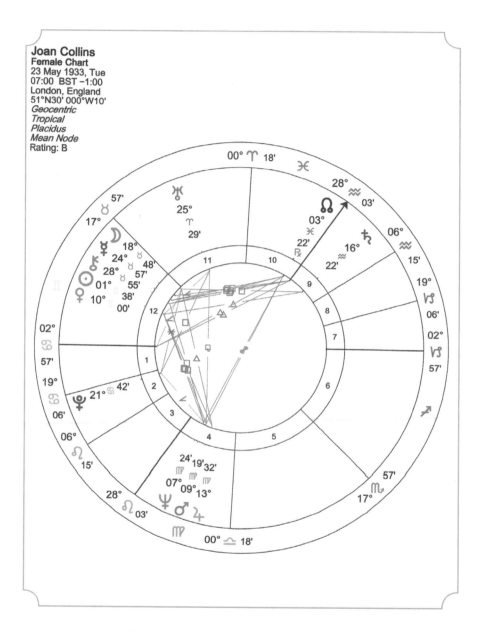

Joan Collins
Female Chart
23 May 1933, Tue
07:00 BST −1:00
London, England
51°N30' 000°W10'
Geocentric
Tropical
Placidus
Mean Node
Rating: B

Nodes of the Moon on Joan Collins's Birth Chart

Parallel and Contra-Parallel

When two planets are at the same level above or below the ecliptic, it is said that they are parallel, and when planets sit one above and one below the ecliptic, they are contra-parallel.

Midpoints

You can take any planet or feature on a chart and look at some other planet or feature and work out the midpoint between the two. This isn't difficult to do by hand but it is a time-consuming job, so let your software do this for you. Midpoints in themselves are sensitive points, and these can become activated if an outer planet makes a major aspect to them. If you happen to have planets two signs apart from each other—for example, Virgo and Scorpio—there will be a collection of midpoints in the sign that lies in the sign that is between them, which in this case is Libra. Any planet that transits Libra or transits in a sign that is opposite (Aries) will have an effect. For other aspects to be felt, one would need a heavy-duty outer planet for it to be really noticeable.

Rectification

Rectification means finding the ascendant when the time of birth is unknown. This isn't an easy thing to do but here are some tips that might help. Let us assume it's your birth time that is vague.

1. If your mother or some other relative is alive, it is worth asking if you were born in hospital, and if so, you could ask if anyone can remember what meal your mother ate after you were born. Hospitals used to feed their patients at 6 a.m., 12 noon, and 6 p.m., so this is often a clue.

2. If you have a vague idea of the time of birth, note down the earliest it could have been and the latest, and make up a chart for the middle of the two times.

3. Think back to some memorable incident in your life, for instance, an accident that landed you in hospital. Now look at the Mc and move it forward by one degree for a year, and see if you can make it form a square or opposition with either Mars or Uranus around the age at which you were when you had the accident. If the aspect registers the accident as happening a couple of years before it actually did, move the Mc back by two degrees and rework the chart for the new Mc position. If the aspect registers the accident as happening two or three years later, move it back to make it fit, then make up a new chart.

4. If the inciting incident was a move of house, a time of illness, a death in the family, a happy time, a wonderful holiday, or anything else, select an appropriate planet and either an easy or a challenging aspect to make it fit.

5. Of course there can be a lot more to it than that. For instance, the transits at the time, or progressions, or even another form of progression called *solar arc progressions* might help.

If the person has no idea of his birth time, set the chart for noon of the birthday and jiggle the Mc back and forth until one connection after another starts to form, then look at transits and progressions for the various unforgettable times.

Degree for a Year Progressions and Solar Arc Progressions

Degree for a year progressions are really easy to do, as it only involves moving everything forward by one degree for each year of life. Solar arc progressions are a little more awkward, as this moves everything forward on the chart by the rate at which the sun progresses, which is 57 minutes of a degree, which itself is just a shade under a degree for a year.

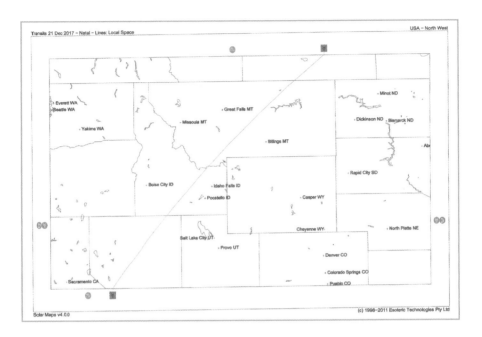

An Example of an Astrocartography Chart

Astrocartography

Astrocartography, or ACG, is a system that came into being in the USA once personal computers became available. The easiest way to understand ACG is to put a large ball on a shelf and shine a flashlight on the front of it. Now, turn the ball slowly to the right and see how the leading edge of the light moves across the surface of the ball. By doing this, you are imitating the effect of the sun shining on the face of the earth.

If you have enough imagination to follow this, you will get the idea. The leading edge of the sun's progress round the earth is the *rise line*; the other edge is the *set line*. If you now imagine a line running up the ball from the point where the sun is brightest, up and over the ball, down the back side of it, under it and back to the brightest spot again, you will be looking at the sun's *Mc line* and imagining the sun's *Ic line*, which is round the back of the ball.

Each of these four lines tells a story, which is like the story of the four main cusps on a birth chart. For instance, the rise line represents the rising sign or

the cusp of the first house, so anywhere that this line falls, shows where you can make an impact. The Ic line is like the cusp of the fourth house, so it represents the chances of a happy home life, while the Mc line shows where you could make a success of a career. The set line is like the cusp of the seventh house, and thus where you can expect to make happy relationships.

The problems become magnified when you consider that we have only looked at the sun so far, but every planet and even the nodes of the moon have to be taken into consideration. So now you have to take into account the nature of each planet. For instance, if you decide to live in a place where Uranus has its Ic line, your home life will be interesting—but also disruptive. If you regularly do business with people in a place where Jupiter is on your Mc line, the work will be successful, but you might be forced to expand your activities too quickly and too much.

There are also *parans* to consider. (Incidentally, we Brits pronounce this word with the emphasis on the first syllable, while Americans put the emphasis on the second syllable.) These are horizontal lines which register that somewhere along the line, a planet is connected with a rise, set, Mc line, or Ic line.

Local Space Astrology

Local space astrology, or LSA, is a much easier concept to understand than ACG. It relates to something called the *altazimuth*, which roughly means "how high and how far" something happens to be. Once again, a bit of imagination is needed. In this case, imagine that at the very moment that a baby is born, it sits up and looks at the planets in the sky, and then draws a line down from each planet in turn, which goes through itself and then carries on around the world.

Each planetary line has a meaning, but unlike the ACG system, you don't have to link a planetary line to a particular aspect of life. Therefore, a Venus line is good for anything and everything, so it isn't limited to your personal image, your home life, your love life, or your career.

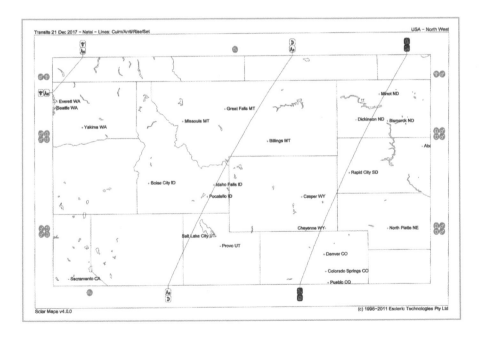

An Example of a Local Space Astrology Chart

Astro Geodetics

This system was used by ancient astrologers to slice up the earth into segments, each being ruled by a different sign. Nowadays, there are several systems in use, some that are relatively simple and others that are extremely complex.

Dignities

Dignities are used in older forms of astrology. The concept is that the planets work better in some signs than others. The system usually involves only the planets that can be seen with the naked eye. There are other divisions of this kind, but this table shows the basic ones:

Planet	Domicile	Exaltation	Fall	Detriment
Sun	Leo	Aries	Libra	Aquarius
Moon	Cancer	Taurus	Scorpio	Capricorn
Mercury	Gemini/Virgo	Virgo	Pisces	Sagittarius/Pisces
Venus	Taurus/Libra	Pisces	Virgo	Aries/Scorpio
Mars	Aries/Scorpio	Capricorn	Cancer	Taurus/Libra
Jupiter	Sagittarius/Pisces	Cancer	Capricorn	Gemini/Virgo
Saturn	Capricorn/Aquarius	Libra	Aries	Cancer/Leo

Traditional and Horary Astrology

This is an older form of astrology that requires a course of study in its own right. It uses the dignities, but also many other factors that are said to influence the way the planets work. The definitive book on this subject is *Christian Astrology* by William Lilly, and it was published in 1647.

Horary astrology is a branch of traditional astrology that gives answers to questions by employing traditional astrological methods. Only the planets that can be seen with the naked eye are used, but the rules for this are complex.

Arabic Parts

Arabic astrology is based on our familiar birth chart, but it uses "parts" and each part is found by a mathematical calculation. For instance, the famous *part of fortune* is found by deducting the position of the sun from that of the

THE PART OF FORTUNE

◆

I have just been reading an interesting interpretation of this, in which the writer suggests it represents the seed of life, the earliest experiences, and even issues carried over from previous lives, along with (in her words) the primal instinct, the unconscious mind, and destiny.

Well, I have always read this part of fortune in a much simpler way, as I consider it to be the point on the chart where a person can make headway fairly easily. It may be the one place where fortune shines on us, even when it doesn't do much shining anywhere else on the chart. I also think the house it occupies is more important than the sign. As a friend whose part of fortune is in her tenth house once told me, "The only fortune I'll ever have is what I get by a lifetime of hard work!"

As you can see from the chart on page 146, President John F. Kennedy's part of fortune was in the fourth house of family and heritage, in the hardworking and ambitious sign of Capricorn.

ascendant and adding the position of the moon, while those born at night must deduct the moon and add the sun. Good-quality software does this for you automatically, and it lists the positions of all the Arabic parts on your chart.

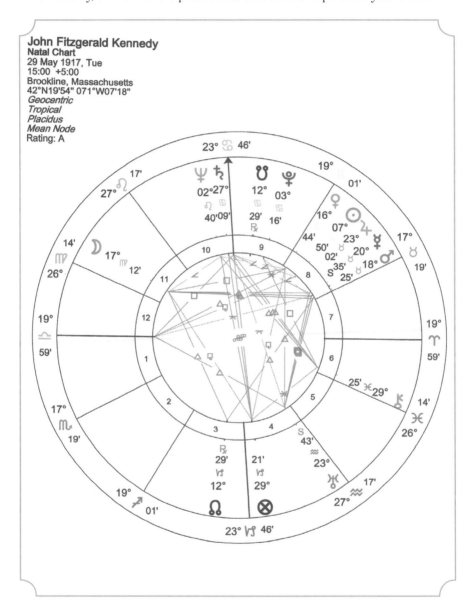

John Fitzgerald Kennedy
Natal Chart
29 May 1917, Tue
15:00 +5:00
Brookline, Massachusetts
42°N19'54" 071°W07'18"
Geocentric
Tropical
Placidus
Mean Node
Rating: A

Part of Fortune

Fixed Stars

This is an ancient name for the stars as opposed to the planets. We know that planets move, but the ancient astrologers considered the stars to be static or fixed. We now know the stars are suns, and that our own sun is a fairly insignificant one that sits on the edge of a galaxy, and that there are trillions of stars, galaxies, and planets all around the universe. As it happens, our galaxy spins and our solar system shifts, so over time, even the fixed stars move.

Precession of the Equinoxes, the Great Ages

The ideas here are somewhat related to the previous paragraph about the fixed stars. The earth wobbles slightly, which has the effect of making the equinoxes and solstices *process* backward in relation to the constellations, to the point where the ascendant moves back by one sign at an interval of 2,000 years. For instance, for the past couple of thousand years, we have been working our way through the Age of Pisces, but one of these days, we will enter the preceding sign, kicking off the Age of Aquarius. Some say this has already happened, perhaps in July 1969 when Neil Armstrong stepped out onto the surface of the moon.

Tropical and Sidereal Astrology

The kind of astrology that we use in the west is called *tropical astrology*, and this links the summer solstice to 0° of Cancer and the winter solstice to 0° of Capricorn, and vice versa in the southern hemisphere. It links to the time when the sun is at its highest in the northern hemisphere, which means it reaches as far north on the face of the earth as the Tropic of Cancer, and to the winter solstice when it reaches as far south as the Tropic of Capricorn.

Sidereal astrology (pronounced sid-ear-ree-al) means the astrology of the stars, as opposed to the astrology of the equinoxes and solstices, which is what Western tropical astrology is based on. This is used in Vedic (Hindu) astrology, which is why one can be a Virgo in our system and a Leo in the Vedic. This confuses (and sometimes even upsets) beginners in astrology, but it shouldn't because Vedic astrology has far more to do with predicting and choosing the right time to do something than character reading.

Other Sensitive Points

We have looked into the vertex, but there is also an anti-vertex, along with east and west points and probably a host of other points now that computers can access them. Some astrologers like to experiment with these.

Asteroids

Now that software can find and list these objects, astrologers are happily experimenting with them, as an addition to the usual planets.

Firmicans, Almutens, and So On

These are mathematical divisions that can be used in some predictive techniques. Some are linked to the dwaads that we saw in the previous chapter.

Hindu/Vedic Astrology

Vedic astrology uses sidereal astrology and it also uses twenty-seven or twenty-eight divisions called *nakshatras*. These are based on the thirteen-degree movement of the moon during the course of a day, and if you divide a circle by this thirteen-degree movement, you get 27.69 degrees, which equates to the twenty-seven or twenty-eight nakshatras. Each nakshatra is named after a god or goddess and has its own character and mythology.

Chinese Astrology

Chinese astrology must have had some kind of link to the solar system and stars way back in the dim and distant past, and there is a theory that it started life not as an examination of what happens on the ecliptic but around the Pole Star. However, there does seem to be some vague connection to the movements of Jupiter and Saturn and those of the sun and moon as well. Some of this is easy to work out by hand once you understand the system, but some is too much of a chore. You can find free-of-charge calculators for this kind of Chinese astrology on the Internet. Each year is ruled by an animal sign.

The Twelve Animal Signs

Rat	Ox	Tiger
Rabbit	Dragon	Snake
Horse	Goat	Monkey
Rooster	Dog	Pig

Each sign is either masculine or feminine, and each is linked to a variety of correspondences. There are also five elements that are used in this astrology, and each element rules for two years. Each element has a variety of links and correspondences.

The Elements				
Wood	Fire	Earth	Metal	Water

The chart is called The Four Pillars because it is split into four columns or pillars, the first showing the animal sign and element for the person's hour of birth, the second for the day of birth, the third for the month of birth, and the fourth for the year of birth.

The system links to the I Ching, Feng Shui, and several other systems, so there is plenty to get your teeth into if you are fascinated by the Orient.

Other Forms of Astrology

No system of astrology is as incomprehensible to Westerners as Aztec astrology, because the language is difficult and the concept is hugely complex. There are calendars for religious use, calendars for farming, and calendars that seem to be used for personal readings, and these can all be put together on one massive (and very beautiful) chart. The Aztecs also use the thirteen-day divisions of the moon and the position of Venus.

Other forms of astrology include Nordic and Celtic Ogham divinations, and there are several more numerology-cum-astrology systems in existence in the Orient.

✳ ✳ ✳

14

ASTROLOGY
IN ACTION

Beginners don't always know how to go about analyzing a birth chart, so the idea here is to take you through the process step-by-step.

Tom Jones–Character and Lifestyle

Let's now analyze the natal chart of a celebrity to show you how to go about it, in this case seeing what we can pick up about character and potential lifestyle. For this exercise I have chosen the chart of Tom Jones, the Welsh singer who is well known in the USA and around the world. He is especially popular in Las Vegas, where he has spent a good deal of his working life. Tom has a strong and melodious baritone voice, and he is known for pop, rock, and blues. When he was younger, his managers marketed him as a sex symbol in much the same way that women are often marketed. He certainly had a good physique and even now that he is past his prime, he still looks after himself well.

Tom was born on June 7, 1940, in Treforest, Pontypridd, which is in Glamorgan in South Wales. The coordinates are 51° 37′ north, 3° 22′ west. Tom was born just after midnight at 00:05 with one hour of British Summer Time (daylight saving).

Tom was born Thomas John Woodward, and his father was a coal miner. The worst time in Tom's life occurred when he was twelve years of age: he became ill with tuberculosis and spent two years in bed recovering with little to do other than listen to music on the radio and draw. This ruined any chances he may have had for a good education, but it developed his imagination and his ambition to become a singer. In the early days, he took jobs in factories to make ends meet, and to make matters even harder, Tom and his girlfriend Linda married at the age of sixteen, a month before their son, Mark Woodward, was born. Linda was also sixteen. Mark is now Tom's manager, and they agree that they are more like brothers than parent and child due to the closeness in their ages.

Tom's marriage lasted up to Linda's death in 2016, although they often lived apart and regardless of Tom's many well-publicized affairs. He admits to having sex with 250 groupies a year when he was at the height of his career! The strange thing is that I have never viewed Tom as a particularly sexy man but as a hardworking entertainer who put his mind to his career and made a success of it. After a great career as a singer, Tom is now a coach on the successful British television show *The Voice*. He comes across as a charming and kindly man who is devoted to music and who prefers to work rather than sit back and retire. So what makes him tick?

Where do we start? Well, it's a good idea to look at the shape of the chart first, and then to start at the ascendant and work your way round the chart in

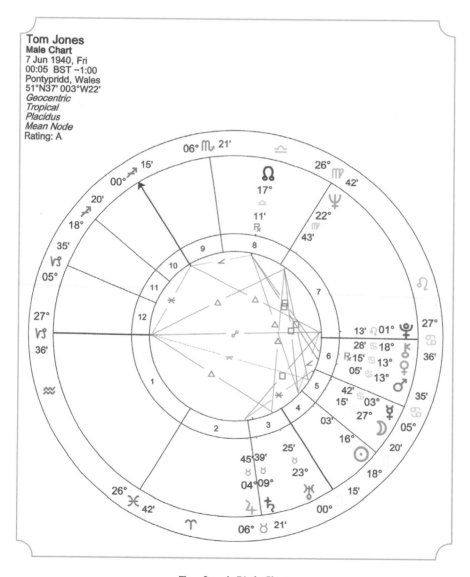

Tom Jones's Birth Chart

a counterclockwise direction, as that way you won't miss anything. In this case, I will give only a brief assessment because that will show you how to go about things without the chapter becoming long-winded and boring.

Weighting

The chart is weighted toward the bottom half, which makes Tom strive to be seen and to be accepted by others. The fact that most of the planets are in the right hemisphere suggests that other people have guided and helped him to become a success. This is a kind of bowl-shaped chart, but there is one planet that sticks out: the creative, imaginative, dreamy, and artistic planet, Neptune. This planet is associated with isolation through illness and a need for a creative outlet.

Rising Sign

Tom's rising sign is Capricorn, which suggests that his family background was one of hard work and poverty, and this was true. It can indicate being brought up or at least looked after by grandparents and other older people, but we don't have any information about that. Capricorn rising endows ambition and thrift, because the person has an instinctive understanding that without money, life can be very hard indeed. The chart has some very large houses, especially the first house, which has the sign of Aquarius intercepted in it. The first house relates to the person and his body, and with Aquarius there, it would show Tom that things can go wrong unexpectedly and that he needs to look after his health and appearance at all times. This lesson seems to have been well learned, since this is not a man who is into gambling, drink, or drugs. In true Capricorn style, he is into hard work, attention to details, and looking after the needs of his family, although his vice was to have lots of girlfriends. Those who have Capricorn rising have a good bone structure and look good even as they age.

The Planets and Nodes

Starting from the ascendant, the first feature is the south node, although not shown here, it is opposite the north node, which is in Libra.. The south node in Aries makes it easy for Tom to be independent and to rely on his own instincts and keep away from dangerous situations. The node is in the second house, making it imperative that he keeps up a good image. The node isn't particularly well starred, so if Tom has lost money along the way through property dealings, it wouldn't be surprising. Capricorn rising is drawn to property matters and the ascendant is in a grand trine with Uranus and Neptune, but the messy situation with the north and south nodes makes speculation in property a poor form of investment for him.

Jupiter is in Taurus, and as Taurus rules the voice and Jupiter brings luck and dazzle to all it touches, this is an important factor. The planet is in the second house of personal wealth, and while it has a difficult square aspect to Pluto, suggesting legal difficulties at some point, it also has a sextile aspect to Mercury, suggesting that business arrangements would be successful.

Saturn is close to Jupiter and is also in Taurus, but while this can be a depressing planet, it favors those who put in the hours and make the effort. As Saturn is in a sign that is associated with music and singing, it is useful to Tom. Saturn is in the third house, as is Uranus, both of which suggest setbacks in his schooling, and we know that his education was severely hindered by his childhood TB.

Tom's sun is in Gemini, which isn't a sign that is especially noted for music, but my guess is that the technical side of creating and recording music would come easily to Tom. Geminis get bored quickly and they like to keep busy, so it isn't surprising that Tom is still working at the age of seventy-seven. The sun is in the fourth house, so Tom's background, family, and even his stay-at-home wife would be important to him. Tom's moon is also in Gemini, which makes him flirtatious. The sun and moon are in a square aspect to Neptune, suggesting a need for artistic expression and a lot of hard work to make it come about. Tom's moon is in the fifth house, which rules love affairs, fun, pleasure, and the good things of life, but it is also a very musical house that brings glamour and wealth as a result of bringing pleasure to others. While I haven't read much about his attitude to his parents, the sun in the fourth house and moon close by suggests Tom took care of his family as soon as he could afford to do so, and we do know that he is close to his son, Mark.

Tom has a stellium (a group of planets) in Cancer, comprising Mercury, Mars, Venus and, Chiron, and while Mercury is in the fifth house, which relates to glamour and show business, the other planets are in the sixth house of work and health. I would guess that if Tom does something for charity, it would be something related to health. He may also be fond of small animals. Interestingly, his Venus is retrograde and square to the nodes, so he must have felt tugged in different directions at times due to his need to work and his desire to be at home or with the family at the same time. The chances are that he now works from home with a studio of his own and a "family" of reliable helpers around him. Mars and Venus being close together makes him pleasant and charming, but not afraid to fight for his rights to be assertive when the need arises. Chiron in the sixth house in Cancer is related to the sickness he had as a child that kept him tied down at home. He may worry about his health or that of his family members.

Pluto on the cusp of the seventh house in Leo shows tragedy in personal relationships, and apart from losing his wife, my guess is that he has lost a number of good friends over the years.

Neptune is an important planet on Tom's chart, as it stands out alone near the top of his chart. Due to the offset nature of the chart, Neptune is in the seventh house, suggesting both help and hindrance from business and other connections, so he must have been swindled at one time or another, and at times it must be hard for Tom to know exactly what others are up to. However, this is a planet of artistry and music, imagination and intuition, so it rules his life, and with its trine to Uranus and the ascendant, Neptune also brings unexpected breakthroughs and doors that open for him just when he most needs them to. Tom tried acting at one point, but it didn't work for him—with Neptune being square to the sun and moon, this isn't surprising. However, while I have no information about this, it wouldn't surprise me to discover that Tom paints for pleasure. I can also see that he is diligent and meticulous in all he does, due to Neptune in Virgo and, of course, that hardworking Capricorn ascendant.

The north node is in Libra, showing Tom that he needs to include others in his plans and that he is better working with others than alone. As a singer and musician, much of his artistic and working life has involved others, so this makes sense. Also, like Taurus, Libra is a sign that is associated with music, so it seems that Tom is doing what he is karmically meant to do with his life.

The midheaven of the chart is in Sagittarius, and this is a very lucky placement for the Mc, as it suggests that Tom would succeed at anything he put his mind to, especially if he was to live and work in a country other than that of his birth. It also suggests a desire to push the boundaries of his ambition and to go as far as he can.

There are many more things that we could find to say about Tom from this chart, but I think this gives you an idea of how to approach things.

❋ ❋ ❋

ABOUT THE AUTHOR

Sasha Fenton wanted to understand what made people tick, and astrology gave her answers. This interest led to a career as a consultant astrologer. Over the years, Sasha has taught astrology, given many lectures, and been broadcast on radio and television across the UK and many other countries. She has lectured and demonstrated at the most prestigious mind, body, and spirit festivals around the world.

Along with thousands of articles and stars columns—most frequently for *Woman's Own* magazine and the Sunday *People* newspaper—Sasha has written 134 books; the latest being a change of direction into her latest Tudorland historical fiction series.

Sasha has served as president of the British Astrological and Psychic Society, as former chair of the British Advisory Panel on Astrological Education, and as a member of the executive council of The Writer's Guild of Great Britain.

Sasha is married to writer and publishing technical advisor Jan Budkowski. She has two children, two adult grandchildren, and two young ones. She lives in the West of England.

IMAGE CREDITS